The New
Complete Book of
TAROT

To Geoff, with love, and to Adriana, in loving memory.

The New Complete Book of

TAROT

A step-by-step guide to reading the cards

Foreword by
Liz Greene

Juliet Sharman-Burke

CONNECTIONS
BOOK PUBLISHING

A CONNECTIONS EDITION
This edition published in Great Britain in 2007 by
Connections Book Publishing Limited
St Chad's House, 148 King's Cross Road
London WC1X 9DH
www.connections-publishing.com

British Library Cataloguing-in-Publication data available on request.

ISBN 978-1-85906-215-9

3 5 7 9 10 8 6 4

The Complete Book of Tarot was previously published by
Penguin Books in the UK and St. Martin's Griffin in the US.

Phototypeset in Albertan and Cochin using QuarkXPress on Apple Macintosh
Printed in China

CONTENTS

Foreword

I n the early 1980s there were few books available on the Tarot. Juliet Sharman-Burke, an experienced Tarot teacher, responded to her students' requests for a correspondence course by creating one, which was then transformed into *The Complete Book of Tarot*. There are now around thirty million references to the Tarot listed on internet search engines, linking the interested individual with interpretations, history both factual and imaginative, newly designed decks of cards, and, of course, books. Most of these books have a brief time in the light and then vanish into oblivion. *The Complete Book of Tarot* has remained popular for the simple reason that it is one of the clearest, most accessible, and least 'doctrinal' of all the many works on these enigmatic cards. Whatever the reader's spiritual views, *The Complete Book of Tarot* addresses the fundamental experiences of human life in a language which both the sophisticated Tarot reader and the individual with little knowledge of the cards can utilise to shed light on the profound underpinnings of meaning in everyday existence.

The cards Juliet used to illustrate the original edition of the book were designed by A. E. Waite in 1910. For many decades these beautiful images were perceived as the 'authoritative' modern deck. But Waite's involvement in Rosicrucian and Theosophical studies infused his creation with a very specific form of spirituality, and the cards did not 'speak' to those unresponsive to such an approach. In 1986 Juliet and I designed a new deck with an accompanying book, called *The Mythic Tarot*. These cards use the narratives of Greek myth to illuminate the psychological patterns and conflicts of everyday human existence. But *The Mythic Tarot's* break from tradition needed to be bridged by a deck that appealed to those who still find the older images evocative. Juliet then designed another, more traditional deck, which draws from both Waite's imagery and older decks such as the fifteenth century Visconti-Sforza cards. It is this new deck, sensitively and beautifully illustrated by Giovanni Caselli, which illustrates *The New Complete Book of Tarot*. The best of all worlds is thus presented in this new edition of the book, which provides both an inspirational and eminently practical path into these mysterious images that have intrigued both scholars and seekers for over five centuries, and will no doubt continue to do so for many centuries to come.

LIZ GREENE
SEPTEMBER 2006

Introduction

This book is intended to give you a comprehensive understanding of the Tarot as well as encouraging your own study and involvement in the learning process. You may want to study the Tarot in order to interpret the cards for others; or you may wish to use it as an aid to personal growth and development. I hope that you will wish to do both.

This book has developed out of many years of teaching Tarot in workshops and by correspondence, so my personal method and style have been reproduced here as much as possible. For instance, I have included 'guided fantasy' exercises because so many students have found them useful in both the memorizing process and in gaining a deeper personal knowledge of each card. Because reading the Tarot relies so heavily on the reader's intuitive and interpretative prowess, it isn't an easy subject to teach. However, I don't believe that any special clairvoyant or psychic powers are needed in order to become a sensitive reader. All of us have natural intuitive powers, and reading the Tarot is certainly one good way of heightening and developing these qualities. The exercises are designed to stimulate the imagination and, in turn, the unconscious powers of intuition. I also found that the idea of the Fool's journey through the Tarot (*see pages 29, 69 and 103*), incorporating myths and legends, caught the students' imagination because they felt able to relate it to their personal stages of growth. The Tarot images are archetypal so the message of each card will touch some aspect of everyone's life, and in learning it you are able to take a fresh look at yourself.

The Tarot is made up of seventy-eight cards. The deck is divided into twenty-two Major Arcana (or Trump) cards and fifty-six Minor Arcana cards. The Major Arcana cards are easily distinguishable by their unusual names and images such as the The Fool, The Magician and The Empress. The remaining fifty-six cards are divided into four suits, rather like our modern playing cards. They are named differently though – Wands, Cups, Swords and Pentacles – and, unlike playing cards, each suit has four Court cards consisting of King, Queen, Knight and Page. In the older decks, the Minor cards have no pictorial images, which makes them quite complicated to learn; however, the Sharman-Caselli deck that Giovanni Caselli and I created in 2000 and which is used for illustration in this book, has images on all the Minor cards, which is helpful for beginners (*see page 22*).

I designed the Sharman-Caselli deck drawing on imagery from two classic decks: the 1910 Waite deck, which became extremely popular partly because it was the first deck to use pictures on the Minor cards, thus making it more accessible; and the Visconti-Sforza Tarot, which is one of the earliest decks, dating back to the mid-fifteenth century. In 1984, I co-designed *The Mythic Tarot* with my good friend and colleague Liz Greene, in which we combined the traditional meanings of the cards with stories from Greek mythology. Our intention was to help make the process of learning the cards easier by using a storyline upon which to hang the divinatory meanings of each card. Both *The Mythic Tarot* and the Sharman-Caselli deck are psychological in orientation and use the idea of the Fool's journey through the stages of life as a backdrop, drawing on the notion that as humans we share collective experiences that are archetypal and are all reflected in the Tarot.

A number of authors have approached the Tarot from a psychological point of view, particularly focusing on the ideas of the Swiss psychoanalyst Carl Gustav Jung, whose theory of the 'collective unconscious' and the four functions of human consciousness are very pertinent to the Tarot, as we shall see as we go along. I, too, have followed Jung's thoughts on stages in life: during the first half of life, concerns with outer life and the development of the personality are paramount, as is searching for happiness and meaning in the material world; during the second half of life, we turn our attention towards the inner world, searching for meaning within rather than without. In order to make the Fool's story of psychological development easier to follow, I have slightly changed the numerical sequence of the Major Trumps. There is considerable controversy among Tarot experts over the numbering of the Major Arcana as the earliest decks weren't numbered and many didn't even have a name;

they just bore the pictorial image. The eighteenth-century occult revival was in fact responsible for much of the rectified numbering (*see page 18*). The Major Arcana of the Sharman-Caselli deck echoes the old style, so the cards have titles but no numbers.

Another relatively modern innovation is that of reading significance into reversed cards. This is a practice to which I do not personally subscribe as, in my opinion, reversals can end up being more confusing and baffling than informative, for each Tarot card carries within its upright position both positive and negative possibilities. Broadly speaking, reversals show the opposite meaning of the upright card, but I believe that both possibilities – along with the surrounding cards in the spread – should always be taken into account. I feel that reversals can act as straightjackets, offering just one solution. For instance, if an upright card reveals 'optimism', its reversed meaning would be 'pessimism'. But I feel that optimism and pessimism sit side by side, not at opposite ends, and both possibilities should always be considered. However, I would encourage you to experiment for yourself at all times, to discover the right path for you. There is no right or wrong way; the most important thing is that you find your own way.

The cards act as springboards from which the intuitive powers should start working, and feelings and ideas evoked by the images are therefore the final touchstone for good divinatory interpretation. The better you get to know your cards – and using the guided fantasy and other exercises described later will help a great deal – the more your intuitive powers will be heightened, and the more sensitive a reader you will become. If, initially, you immerse yourself in the stories of the cards, they will filter through into your unconscious so you'll find that you are able to interpret the cards intuitively rather than needing to refer to the book to discover what each card means. As the old saying goes, the more you sow, the more you will reap.

I have divided the book into four sections. The first three explain the cards in detail, and each ends with some suggested exercises. The fourth section concentrates on interpretation and describes how to conduct a reading. I have included a number of sample readings to illustrate possible style and interpretation. The book has been arranged in such a way as to weave together the learning process and the path of self-discovery. The Major and Minor cards are mixed together in each section to encourage equal interest in both, for what often seems to happen is that the twenty-two Major Trumps are learned first, and, as they can be used quite successfully on their own, the task of learning the other fifty-six cards tends to get put off. This is a pity because the Minor cards are an extremely valuable addition to the Tarot, as you will see as we go along. If you follow the sections in turn and complete all the exercises as suggested, you will be surprised at how quickly and naturally you will come to grips with the ancient art of Tarot reading.

The Origins of the Cards

Almost as fascinating and mysterious as the Tarot cards themselves is the mystery surrounding their historical origins and purpose. While it is true that the Tarot was, and still is, used as a game, it is also clear that the human love of playing games exists alongside an equally human desire to understand and reveal the unknown. The Tarot can be used as a way of gaining knowledge and insight regarding the past, present and future. Indeed, games are an interesting model for life – the cards we are dealt involve a certain amount of luck but how we play the hand is up to us. Whether the Tarot cards were originally designed as a game or a symbolic system for divination, and whether the Major and Minor cards were designed separately (and, if so, when they came together) is still ambiguous, even after much research and debate. Arthur E. Waite, himself a significant figure in the Tarot's history, wrote in the preface of *Le Tarot des Bohémiens*, 'The chief point regarding the history of the Tarot cards, whether used as pretexts for fortune telling or as symbols of philosophical interpretation, is that such history does not in fact exist.'[1]

Although there are many books on the possible origins of the Tarot, written by historians for academic purposes and lovers of Tarot alike, there is still no definitive answer. Many different theories exist as to the Tarot's geographical and philosophical roots – its beginnings have been attributed to Italy, Spain, Southern France, the Far East, the Middle East and Egypt, among other places – and many of these theories are fascinating and compelling. Indeed, it is part of the Tarot's richness that it has elements in common with so many different countries and their myths and legends; the possibilities are as interesting as whatever the reality might be, so I will touch on a few of them here.

Some writers have speculated that the cards come from India and that the Minor Arcana refer to the four castes of Hinduism: Cups to the

[1] Encausse, Gérard, 'Papus', *Le Tarot des Bohémiens*, Paris, 1889

priests or Brahmins; Swords to the warriors or Kshatriyas; Coins or Pentacles to the merchants or Vaisyas; and Rods or Wands to the serfs or Sudras. The Major Arcana has been linked with Buddhism: the Fool could be the wandering monk whose path of enlightenment parallels the path taken by the Tarot Fool.

Moving to Europe: a monk named Brother Johannes of Bredfeld in Switzerland[1] wrote an essay in 1377 describing a game of cards that outlined society's structure. He declared that he was ignorant of when it was invented, where and by whom, but he suggested the cards portrayed kings, noblemen and commoners, and could therefore be used for moral purposes to map out a society and its structure. It could then teach people the lesson of knowing and keeping to their place. The suits represented the classes of society: Cups for the church; Swords for the aristocracy; Coins or Pentacles for the merchants; and Rods or Wands for the peasants. Staying in Europe: evidence exists from a court ledger of King Charles V1 of France stating that money had been paid to Jacquemin Gringonneur for three packs of cards illustrated in 'gold and diverse colours ornamented with many devices', which sound suspiciously like early Tarot cards.

The Tarot first appeared in the form we know it in Italy during the mid fifteenth century. Richard Cavendish suggests that the Tarot Trumps may have emerged from the prevailing Renaissance background, which was of interest in the use of pictures as 'instructional, magical and mnemonic devices.'[2] The Renaissance humanists believed that the profound wisdom of the ancient world – a blend of Pythagoreanism, Graceo-Egyptian gnosticism and Hermetic and Cabalistic teachings – underpinned many different spiritual and esoteric traditions. Cavendish postulates that imagery drawn from this background found its way into the Tarot Trumps.

Another theory put forward by Jessie Weston in her book *From Ritual to Romance*[3] is that the Tarot emblems of the Wand, Cup, Sword and Pentacle were connected with the four Grail Hallows or sacred

[1] Tilley, Roger. *Playing Cards*, Octopus Books, 1973
[2] Cavendish, Richard. *The Tarot*, Michael Joseph, 1975
[3] Weston, Jessie. *From Ritual to Romance* (first pub. 1920), Anchor Books, 1957

objects found in the Grail castle of Arthurian legend. An interesting combination of Judaeo-Christian symbols and mysterious Celtic images emerged in the Grail romances, which appeared between 1180 and 1200, and took European culture by storm. Like the Tarot, the Grail legends reflect a path of personal development and integration that makes it clear they are not merely stories but are symbolic of the process of striving towards self-awareness and illumination. Weston proposed that such arcane wisdom was a secret of the fourteenth-century Knights Templar who were believed to be privy to the inner mystery of the Grail. The Tarot suits and Grail Hallows couple thus:

WAND The Lance of Longinus, the Roman centurion who was said to have pierced Christ's side as He hung from the Cross.

CUP The Grail itself, said to be the cup used by Jesus at the Last Supper.

SWORD King David's legendary Sword of the Spirit referred to in the Old Testament.

PENTACLE The Plate from which the Last Supper was eaten.

The four Grail Hallows could be seen, in turn, to have descended from the Four Treasures of Ireland, the magical emblems of Celtic myth. These treasures were said to have belonged to the pre-Christian Celtic gods known as the Tuatha de Danaan or the People of the Goddess Danu. The chieftains of the Tuatha were expected by their people to maintain wellbeing and prosperity of the land through their supernatural powers. Four magical treasures, the Spear of Lug, the Cauldron of the Dagda, the Sword of Nuada and the Stone of Fal aided the gods in this. These four treasures show striking similarities to the four Grail Hallows, and, in turn, to the four Tarot suits.

WAND The Spear of Lug is named after a supremely versatile god who was known among his people for being 'many skilled'. Legend goes that when he presented himself to the Tuatha de Danaan, wishing to join them, he was asked to state his craft. Lug replied, 'Carpenter', and was duly informed that the Tuatha already had a carpenter. Lug added that he was also a smith, and was told they already had a smith, too. Lug then announced that he was not only a carpenter and a smith, but also a warrior, a harpist, a historian, a poet, a sorcerer, a hero and many other things beside. Each post was reputedly already filled, but when Lug demanded to know whether the court had a single member who possessed all these skills, it seemed they had not, so the triumphant Lug was finally admitted to join the Tuatha de Danaan. When we come to look closely at the 'flavour' of each suit, we will see how admirably this tale fits in with the suit of Wands and its element, fire.

CUP The Cauldron of the Dagda, meaning the All-Father, could never be emptied, and no-one was left with his hunger unsatisfied. The Dagda was known as the nourisher of all his people, and his inexhaustible cauldron not only fed the hungry but was even able to bring the dead back to life. This treasure is connected with the Cups, and their element, water.

SWORD The deadly Sword of Nuada, King of the Tuatha, was so powerful that, when unsheathed, no enemy could ever escape it. The suit of Swords, often associated with strife and battle, connects with this treasure. The Swords' element, air, fits well as it is the element that seeks to find the inescapable truth.

PENTACLE The Stone of Fal, the coronation seat of Irish Kings, was said to cry out loud when sat upon by the rightful King of Ireland. The stone of St Columba, a cross-patterned stone found in old Celtic churchyards, seems to have connections with the Stone of Fal, which, like the stone of St Columba, was found floating magically upon water. The Siege Perilous is the Arthurian equivalent of the chair in which only the true High Prince could be safely enthroned. This treasure combines the earthy with the magical, both qualities attributed to the Pentacles and their element, earth.

If we take each element and suit as representative of a psychological function, as conceived of by Carl Jung, we can elaborate on the basic energies contained in each card. Let us look at each suit, element and psychological function in turn.

Wands ~ Fire ~ Intuition

Fire is the energy that, in psychological terms, is called intuition. It is the spark of divine creativity, the feeling of inspiration and inner certainty that forms an important beginning for the whole creative process. Fire is the faith in one's ability to have 'brainwaves', and to be able to make something out of a passing thought or daydream. Intuition is connected with the imagination and the world of creative fantasy. However, without the other elements – water, air and earth – to balance and stabilize this energy, it's possible that the creativity may fizzle out through lack of form. Associations to the motifs of flames, salamanders and positive colours of red, orange, and yellow will help you to identify the element and its message.

Cups ~ Water ~ Feeling

Water symbolizes the feelings and emotions that give depth to the creative urge represented by fire. Whereas fire is active, masculine, life-giving power, the energy provided by water is passive, feminine, nurturing. Water represents the feelings and emotions that are constantly shifting expression. In the suit of Cups, the water element seems to refer mainly to relationships and personal life. When working together, the suit and its element deal with inner experiences and realities that are emotional and therefore illogical and volatile. In the same way that uncontained fire may burn out of control and become destructive, so uncontained water may overwhelm and end up drowning that which is most valuable within. The themes of fish, mermaids, streams, rivers and fountains help identify the element of water, as do the soft colours of watery blues and pale pinks.

Swords ~ Air ~ Thinking

The Swords, the suit traditionally connected with strife and difficulty, represent the element of air. Air and intellect seek out truth and logic, and the cutting edge of the thought process depicted by the Swords can slice through deception and illusion even though this may sometimes be painful. However, if things are seen and understood, and even accepted, then choices can be made and decisions taken. Thinking is an essential function which we use to sort out muddled emotions; the more confused we become, the more we need the sharp edge of the Swords to cut through to the truth. The design of birds and butterflies as well as an emphasis on cloud formation run through the Swords as a memory theme. The cool colours of ice blues, greys and pale mauves act as a reminder of the airy element.

Pentacles ~ Earth ~ Sensation

Earth is a symbol for our bodies, our physical being and our physical needs. The earth itself provides the firm base from which we can grow. From the intuitive conception of an idea (fire), through its emotional importance (water), tested by the intellect (air), the earth finally provides a container for the idea to develop into reality. The element earth is the essential base on which foundations for creative, emotional or intellectual ideas can be established. These can be made solid and brought to concrete form through the earth-plane or sensation function. The symbol of the five-pointed star, which is engraved on each pentacle, is a magical glyph symbolizing the earthy magic that is found every day in our bodies, in nature and in our world. The themes that typify the element of earth are small animals, flowers and fruit, which all signify the earth's bounty. The colours are greens and browns, reminiscent of the natural world.

More recently, Tarot expert Paul Huson has painstakingly traced the origins of the four suits of the Minor Arcana, via the surviving Mamluk decks of Egypt, to the heraldic symbols denoting the four virtues and the four Mazdean castes of ancient Persia.[1] He suggests that the four cardinal virtues of Prudence, whose emblem is a circular mirror, Justice, who carries a sword, Temperance, whose symbol is a cup, and Fortitude, who carries a rod or wand, can be linked with the four suits of the Minor Arcana, namely Pentacles, Swords, Cups and Wands. These four virtues also appear in the Major Arcana: The Hermit as Prudence; Justice; Temperance; and Strength as Fortitude.

Huson also locates the figures of the Major Arcana in the mystery and miracle plays that were popular in the Middle Ages. Mystery plays were supernatural dramas or sacred histories that were played out before followers of Christianity. The play would start with the birth of a hero, follow his life, then chart his death or descent into darkness to retrieve some treasure. This might be in the form of a loved one or even the hero's own life. The hero must struggle in the dark before winning the prize and returning to life or the outer world in triumph. Of course, the life, death and triumphant rebirth of Jesus was the play most popular in Europe during the Middle Ages, but such miracle plays had their roots in the mystery plays of ancient Greece. Among such plays were the Eleusian mysteries, which celebrated over two years the abduction of Persephone, her restoration to Demeter, the birth, life and violent death of Dionysus, Persephone's impregnation and Dionysus' rebirth as Iacchus, god of light.

Although the Tarot made its first documented appearance in Renaissance Italy in the fifteenth century, it enjoyed a major revival in the eighteenth century, when French occultists claimed its origins to be Egyptian. They declared that it contained the purest doctrines of Egyptian priests, who were said to have concealed secrets in the images of the cards to protect and preserve them from the uninitiated. They put forward the theory that the cards had been brought into Europe by gypsies, who were then believed to have emigrated from Egypt. The pioneer in this school of thought was Antoine Court de Gebelin, a clergyman

[1] Huson, Paul, *Mystical Origins of the Tarot*, Destiny Books, 2004

who was deeply interested in the secret lore and doctrines of ancient Egypt. This subject enjoyed fashionable attention at the time, along with all kinds of other esoteric and occult matters. Court de Gebelin thought the Tarot images of the Major Arcana were remnants of the Book of Thoth, and wrote a highly acclaimed book entitled *The Primitive World Analysed and Compared with the Modern World*[1] in which he connected the Major Arcana with secret beliefs and traditions of ancient Eygpt. According to Court de Gebelin, the ancient custom was to stand in the temples of Thoth, whose walls were adorned with pictorial images representing the major forces governing the patterns of life. The person wishing to consult the gods would throw a loose bundle of rods at random, and as they fell with varying emphasis towards one image or another, the priests would interpret the patterns, which were known as 'the words of the gods'. Out of this custom grew the practice of carrying the images around in card form, 'the unbound leaves of the sacred book of Thoth Hermes Trismegistus'. In this way, consultation with the gods became much less complicated and any room could be turned into a temple, simply by producing the pack of cards.

In the nineteenth century, a French Rosicruician and cabalist Eliphas Levi stressed the apparent link between the twenty-two letters of the Hebrew alphabet and the twenty-two cards of the Major Arcana. The Major cards were renumbered to fit into this cabalistic system and many modern packs follow the numerical order of this time. The letters of the Hebrew alphabet were said to connect with the twenty-two paths of the cabalistic Tree of Life, which, among other things, illustrates how the world came into being through the ten divine emanations or spheres that correspond to the Minor Arcana cards, Ace to Ten. The four suits were connected with the Hebrew letters of the alphabet, Y-H-V-H, which denoted the great name of God. The letters were in turn connected with each of the four elements thus: Y, fire and the suit of Wands signifies the initial spark of creative energy that is needed to start any project or living thing; the first H, Water and Cups adds emotion and feeling to this

---

[1] Court de Gebelin, Antoine. *Le Monde Primitif Analysé et Comparé avec le Monde Moderne*, Paris, 1781

process, but until V, Air and Swords, standing for intellect and power of thought, is added, the energy and emotions remain unorganized. The final H, Earth and Pentacles stands for the operation of making the end product real in physical terms by giving it structure and form.

In the late nineteenth century, the Hermetic Order of the Golden Dawn gave the Tarot an important position in its teaching and has proved to be a major influence on subsequent attempts to interpret the cards. Although the order only lasted a couple of years, it nevertheless exercised a lasting effect on subsequent magical groups. The Golden Dawn's ancestry went back to the Rosicrucians, whose secret wisdom had its roots in cabala. Their teachings included alchemy, aspects of Graeco-Egyptian Gnosticism and magic. Arthur Edward Waite joined the Golden Dawn in 1891 and devised the Waite deck drawn by Pamela Colman-Smith, which is one of the most popular decks around today. Other well-known members of the order included the notorious magician Aleister Crowley, who also designed his own Tarot deck, and W. B. Yeats, who was fascinated by the use of Tarot cards to explore mysterious worlds and evoke visions, a technique taught by the Golden Dawn.

Today the Tarot is used for divination but also for self-illumination and exploration; a system that has been around for at least five hundred years yet shows no sign of ageing. Indeed, its popularity seems to be increasing, but it's not losing any of its mysterious appeal. More new decks are being designed all the time, and many of the oldest ones are being rediscovered and printed, while research continues into the history and origins of the enigmatic cards.

How the Tarot Works

T he riddle of why the Tarot cards work lies within the mind of the reader rather than in the actual cards. The images act as mirrors, which offer a reflection of unsuspected knowledge buried deep in the unconscious mind. Rachel Pollack[1] says that while ancient people spoke of the 'other worlds' or the 'lands of the gods', today we speak of the 'unconscious'. She points out that the underlying experience remains: a realm of being in which time does not exist and knowledge is not limited to the images received from our senses. The Tarot works as a bridge between our conscious and unconscious knowledge. Answers and knowledge arise out of the unconscious through dream, fantasy and intuition, and, when sensitively read, the Tarot cards stimulate this intuition.

Paul Huson[2], a respected Tarot authority, suggests that learning the meanings of the pictorial images on the cards can be compared with, or possibly even arose from, ancient memory systems or 'ars memorativa'. The Greeks invented an art of memory system based on impressing upon the mind a sequence of images with a particular significance, to improve memory recall. This method was passed on via the Romans, and was used a great deal by medieval monks. In the days when books were rare and costly, student monks were obliged to memorize lengthy tracts from the few available books and manuscripts. To aid their memory, they used pictures or specially arranged symbols around which to focus each section of the text. The material would be mentally filed away, as it were, under the 'heading' of the particular image or picture, in the back of the student's mind. Whenever a particular chapter or tract needed to be retrieved, the student would simply look at the appropriate key image, and the knowledge would automatically come forward to his conscious mind. This system was used to memorize religious creeds, and the practice of following the Stations of the Cross in Catholic churches is an example of this system still in use today.

1 Pollack, Rachel. *Seventy-Eight Degrees of Wisdom*, The Aquarian Press, 1983
2 Huson, Paul. *The Devil's Picturebook*, Abacus, 1971

However, the monks did not include one special practice, which had been a central part of classical memory systems. This was a Greek method of approaching gods called the 'enlivening' of the imagination, believed to bring additional mysterious benefits as well as an excellent memory. During the Italian Renaissance, when the Tarot first emerged in the form it retains today, memory systems started to include associations with magical talismans, amulets or pictures, which it was hoped would reveal the deeper meanings behind the whole of creation. Meditation upon these profound images was intended to raise an individual's consciousness beyond the mundane and the trivial in order to achieve a connection with the divine.

In many ways, learning to read the Tarot works in a similar way to the 'ars memorativa'. Using the images on the cards to enrich and enliven the imagination, the reader gains a special insight into the cards and their meanings. By learning the symbols on each card in this way, the associations will spontaneously reveal themselves each time a card is laid out. The Tarot images act like mirrors, reflecting things that the unconscious mind already knows, and feeding this information through to the conscious mind. Those images are powerful archetypes that can identify relevant associations with unexpected accuracy if left to their own devices.

The imagery on the Major Arcana of the Sharman-Caselli deck, which is used to illustrate this book, uses colour and symbolism to aid understanding of the cards, but you will notice that various key images keep recurring. For example, the colours white and red represent the opposition between intellect and emotion, while the frequent appearance of two pillars reminds us of the continual tension between the opposites of youth and age, day and night, life and death, masculine and feminine. The Minor Arcana uses key colours to alert the reader instantly to the elements of each suit: reds and yellows for the fiery Wands; soft blues and pinks for the watery Cups; ice blue and grey for the airy Swords; and greens and browns for the earthy Pentacles. By the same token there are recurring symbols, such as salamanders and flames for fire, fish or mermaids to signify water, birds and butterflies for air, and fruit and animals to represent earth.

Getting to Know Your Cards

⁂

Getting to know your Tarot deck is a vital part of the process of understanding the Tarot. Although the Sharman-Caselli deck is used to illustrate this book, the divinatory meanings will work with any deck, so you should choose the pack you like best. The images need to appeal to your personal taste and sense of style and colour, for the pictures must be impressive enough for you to turn them into 'mind mirrors'. The old superstition that buying your own pack is unlucky can be safely ignored. The most important thing is that you feel at home with your cards; they should be like old friends, intimate and familiar – this may not be achieved with a pack that you've been given. There are hundreds of decks to choose from, from the traditional fifteenth-century Visconti or the woodcut Marseilles deck, to the more modern Waite deck, through to the imaginative decks like the Mythic Tarot or the Arthurian Tarot. It is well worth taking some time to decide your preference as, once you start working with one set of images, it's difficult to switch to another.

Having chosen a deck, examine the images carefully: the exciting process of getting to know the cards is just beginning. Treat your cards with respect; treasure them as something special to you alone, and try not to let other people handle them casually. Some readers keep their cards in a little box; others wrap them in a cloth. I use the traditional black silk square, which was believed to keep the cards neutral and protect them from negative energies. Whether or not you believe this, the real importance lies in the care and effort you take in making and keeping a relationship with your cards. Anything we treasure takes on a special significance and this applies to your Tarot cards.

Many Tarot readers prepare for a reading using a method of relaxation such as a series of breathing exercises. The rhythm of deep breathing relaxes the body and, in turn, the mind, so that the intuitive powers are free to come to the fore. It is helpful to work out, and stick to, a preparatory routine, which will help you to distinguish your individual style.

It is important to use imagination and fantasy to get to know your cards and interpret their images so that the intuitive levels of the unconscious are stirred. A good way to do this is to make up stories about each card, letting your imagination revolve around the chosen image. If you do this several times, you will find that the card starts to automatically produce its own associated images. Make a note of the images that recur. Acquiring this habit can increase your personal feeling about each card as you build your own rapport with the images. Let yourself really *feel* the heat of the blazing Sun; let the cool mist rising from the dewy pond on the Moon card send shivers down your spine; *smell* the fresh summer's scent in the Empress's cornfield; *hear* the loud blast from the Judgement angel's trumpet. This all helps to enliven your imagination. It may seem an effort at first, but if you are serious in your wish to become a good Tarot reader, you cannot afford to take short cuts. Once you get involved in the enchanted work of imagination and fantasy, it will become too much fun to seem like work.

To develop as a truly sensitive Tarot reader you must be serious in your intention. You need to be aware of what your cards can and can't do for you. They can give indication and guidelines for future events, they can clarify a difficult situation, which makes it possible for you to start thinking about it in a different light, and they can suggest opportunities for change or action. The energy of the cards seems to indicate the possibilities available, but you need to meet them halfway. Just as it's no good sitting inside when the sun is shining, hoping to get a tan, the energies and opportunities indicated by the cards have to be acted upon. If the cards suggest change, do something positive about it. If they suggest you do nothing, take heed. One client came for a reading to ask for advice about a complication that had arisen during a house purchase. The cards indicated that it wasn't a good proposition, and that it would prove too much for him to cope with. However, the client took no notice, proceeded with the legal battles and finally bought the house, only to find that he couldn't manage the payments and was forced to sell almost immediately. He consulted me over the next purchase and that time the cards were more favourable. As far as I know, he is still living in the second house.

A common difficulty when first reading for friends, is the temptation to prejudge situations. This happened to me long ago when I was learning to read Tarot. A work colleague asked me to read her cards to see if she would ever marry. This woman was much older than I was and she had wanted to marry for a long time but had had no successful relationships. She was in her forties and, from my youthful naive position, I personally doubted that she would ever marry. I was reluctant to even do the reading as I didn't want to be the bearer of bad tidings, so when the cards indicated love, marriage and a change of residence I was surprised and essentially disbelieving, so much so that I was tempted not to tell her what I saw to avoid disappointment, so sure was I that I knew best. Nevertheless, I read the cards truthfully, and three days after the reading she met the man that she was to marry six months later, and moved to another country. This is a prime example of how difficult it can be to suspend your own judgement, and yet it is a necessary lesson to learn.

However, what the cards will not do is state definite, unchangeable events. Their message is often necessarily vague, for it's important to give the seeker room to make up their own mind. Specific questions are very difficult to answer, and the cards should be used as a guide rather than as a set of strict instructions. When dealing with difficult matters in a reading, try to discuss what can be done and how the situation may have arisen rather than attempting to offer concrete predictions or advice. Sometimes, just acknowledging that difficulties exist can be helpful. Tarot readers are often consulted by clients who are in a state of confusion, indecision or despair, both mentally and emotionally. They may turn to the cards for help when they have a problem to solve, so be prepared to listen as well as to talk. Sample readings in the fourth part of the book suggest how this can be done.

The following sections give full descriptions of each card, their symbolic descriptions and their meaning within a reading. Be sure to follow the sections systematically and perform all the exercises completely before moving on to the next stage. The sections have been formulated to make the learning process simple and enjoyable as well as a way of slowly building an in-depth knowledge.

PART ONE

MAJOR CARDS

The Fool

The Magician

The Empress

The Emperor

The High Priestess

The Hierophant

The Lovers

The Chariot

✢

MINOR CARDS

The Aces

The Twos

The Threes

The Fours

The Fives

The Fool's Journey

I would like to treat the Major Trumps in terms of the Fool's journey through various stages of life, a familiar theme in a great many myths, legends and fairy tales. The Fool's journey can be seen as a story that makes the Tarot easier to learn and understand, especially because this theme is, broadly speaking, that of everyone's life. The basic myth starts with the birth of a hero, a person with mortal and divine parentage. In our story, the hero is the Fool and in Section One we will follow his early life through childhood and education (The Magician), meeting his mortal parents (The Empress and The Emperor) his divine parents (The High Priestess and The Hierophant) and his loves and conflicts (The Lovers and The Chariot).

The Tarot images are archetypal, as is the story this journey tells, and some myths and legends overlap. As many mythological figures have much in common with specific cards, I have found it useful to associate the Major Arcana cards with a particular mythical story or figure and, on the whole, I have stuck to Greek myths as their richness provides a good sense of the card, its meanings and its resonances. The myth of the Judgement of Paris, for example, adds a much richer dimension to The Lovers card than its bald keyword description 'a love affair involving a trial or choice'.

The four elements of fire, water, air and earth, which feature so prominently in astrology, alchemy and the whole spectrum of esoteric thought, also appear frequently in Tarot imagery. Some, though not all, of the cards can be associated with zodiac signs or their planets, and, when appropriate, I have included them.

Let us now look at the first eight cards in detail, starting with The Fool.

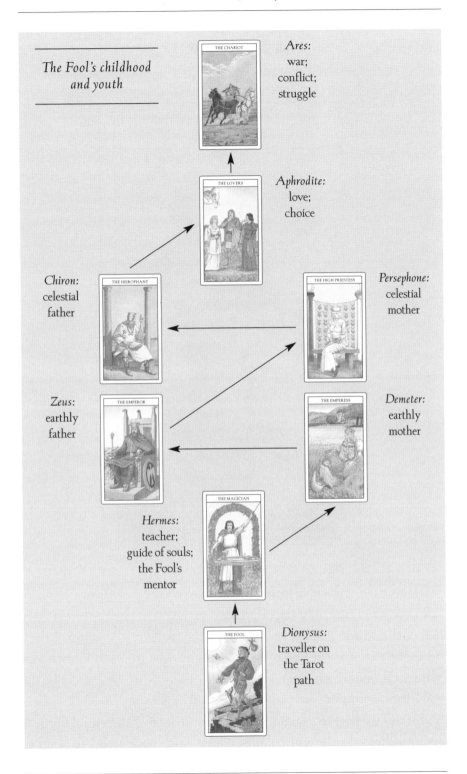

The Fool's childhood
and youth

Ares:
war;
conflict;
struggle

Aphrodite:
love;
choice

Chiron:
celestial
father

Persephone:
celestial
mother

Zeus:
earthly
father

Demeter:
earthly
mother

Hermes:
teacher;
guide of souls;
the Fool's
mentor

Dionysus:
traveller on
the Tarot
path

· THE FOOL ·

The image of the Fool starts off the Major Arcana sequence. In many ways he is the most important card in the pack. The Fool is the only one of the Major Arcana to live on in the modern playing card deck where he exists as the Joker. The Joker in modern games is known as a 'wild' card, one which can take the place of any other card and, like the Tarot Fool, is unnumbered and can mean all or nothing.

Let us take time to examine the imagery in depth. The central figure is a youth dressed in bright colours, whose open pose seems to want to embrace the world. He shoulders a staff with a bag attached to it, and holds before him a single white rose. His upturned, cheerful face and confident posture suggest energy and adventure. A dog prances beside him looking both excited and anxious as together they prepare to step off the edge of the imposing precipice. This is the first step of the Fool's journey into the unknown, yet his expression is calm and positive. The cliff edge is at the forefront, so we can't see what lies beneath the Fool; the Fool doesn't even look. Behind him in the distance lies a dark forest, but a bright sun fills the left-hand corner of the card and the figure of the Fool seems to rise above the clouds.

The Fool carries his staff and bundle lightly; it doesn't appear to be a heavy burden. The bundle represents his past experiences of which he has no immediate need. The staff symbolizes energy, yet the Fool carries it nonchalantly over his shoulder as if he is unaware of or unimpressed by its powerful potential. Before the Fool flutters a beautiful butterfly, a symbol of the psyche and the truth, which is perhaps what the Fool seeks. In the forefront of the card is a laurel bush; perhaps it is the one that supplies the leaves from which the crown on the figure of the World, the final card, is fashioned. The Fool wears bright multi-coloured clothes, reflecting the muddled impulses within him that pull him in different directions. His dog symbolizes the instinctive fear of the unknown that all humans share, while his step off the edge of the precipice shows that, despite his fear, he is prepared to take the plunge into uncharted terrain.

In this Tarot tale, the Fool is our hero. The figure of the Fool could be associated with a number of Greek, Egyptian or Celtic heroes, many of whom have a similar story. Born of both mortal and divine parents, the hero follows a quest that involves him facing many different situations, including conquering the forces of darkness before achieving his goal in triumph. The character of Dionysus, the Greek god of wine, has much in common with the Tarot Fool. He was known as an overturner of hidebound traditions, the god of madness as well as ecstasy. One myth tells that Dionysus was born of the union between Zeus and Semele, a mortal. However, when Zeus's jealous wife Hera discovered that Semele was carrying her husband's child, she disguised herself as the girl's maid and persuaded Semele to insist that Zeus reveal himself to her in all his divine glory. When he did so, she was immediately scorched to death by brilliance too great for mortal flesh to behold. Nevertheless, Zeus managed to save the unborn Dionysus and sealed the foetus in his thigh until it was ready to be delivered. When the baby Dionysus was finally born, Zeus entrusted him to Hermes' care and upbringing. Another Orphic version of the birth of Dionysus tells that the Titans, older gods envious of Dionysus' noble birth, tore him limb from limb and boiled him in a cauldron. Zeus, however, stepped in again, saving the child's heart, which he fed to Persephone, queen of the underworld, in the form of pomegranate seeds. Thus impregnated, Persephone gave birth to Dionysus-Zagreus, god of light and ecstasy.

The Fool is like each of us on our various quests through life. He is like the child discovering life for the first time, or the adult searching for a new meaning or sense of purpose. The Fool seeks the truth, and turns his attention towards the spirit in search of it. His madness or foolishness links him to the divine, for originally the word 'silly' meant 'blessed'. The Fool is simple, trusting, innocent and ignorant of the trials and pitfalls that await him; he is prepared to abandon his old ways and take the leap into the unknown in order to follow his quest.

Perhaps you can identify with the Fool as you begin your adventure and prepare to journey with him through the Tarot. Like him, you are moving into unfamiliar territory, not knowing where it may lead you. Learn with him as he travels the various paths of knowledge, development and self-awareness.

When The Fool appears in a reading, you may be sure that an unexpected influence will soon come into play. There may be a sudden opportunity, or the possibility of adventure or escape. The Fool represents the need to abandon the old ways and start something new and untested. Anything could happen, so hold your nose and jump!

· The Magician ·

THE MAGICIAN

The Magician is the first person the Fool encounters on his journey through life. The image on the card shows a young, dark-haired man dressed in a white tunic and a scarlet cloak. White signifies his inner purity, and red is a symbol of his purposeful activity. He stands beneath an arch of red and white roses. These colours also represent masculine and feminine, or passion and purity, which exist in harmony within him. His belt, which is a snake eating its own tail, symbolizes eternity, and the lemniscates, or figures of eight, that decorate the edge of table, stand for infinity. The Magician holds one hand up, and is pointing a wand heavenwards to symbolize the purity of his higher aspirations, while the other hand points downwards, for he is a link between the gods and men, spirit and matter. His pose suggests that what is above is mirrored by what is below. Before him on a table stand four objects: a wand, a cup, a sword and a pentacle.

The Magician is often compared with Hermes, the Greek messenger god, who was an extremely versatile and flexible character. Not only did he carry messages between the gods and men, he also acted as a protector to men on all their journeys. And as, in ancient times, most journeys were undertaken for commercial purposes, he also became known as the god of merchants and thieves. In his more sombre role of psychopomp he was expected to accompany men on their final journey as he guided the souls of the dead to the underworld. His versatile intellect earned him the title of god of education and the mind, yet he was also a trickster, enjoying mischievous pranks on gods and men alike,. But he always remained popular with both on account of his good nature. He was entrusted with the delivery of his half-brother Dionysus and kept him safe from jealous Hera who wanted to kill her husband's illegitimate offspring. In the Tarot story, the Magician takes care of the Fool.

The objects laid out on the Magician's table correspond with the four suits of the Minor Arcana, and also with the four elements – fire, water air and earth – which in ancient times were thought to form the world. They can also correspond with the Jungian four functions of consciousness: intuition, feeling, thinking and sensation, and in turn can be linked with the attributes of Hermes; Wands with the caduceus, his herald's staff of office that all respected; Cups with the cup of fortune that Hermes gave mortals to sip from in order to change their fortune in love; Swords with the sword given to him by Zeus with which to slay Argos, the many-eyed monster; and Pentacles with the coin symbolizing his guise as protector of merchants and thieves. Hermes was granted the powers of divination by Apollo, which earned him the title of Lord of the Tarot. All manner of divination came under Hermes' jurisdiction, including ancient methods using each of the four elements to foretell the future: pyromancy – divination by fire; hydromancy – divination by water; aeromancy – divination by air; and geomancy – divination by earth.

The Magician stands for a teacher-guide, a person who offers education and enlightenment to all pupils attending the first lesson in the school of life. The energy embodied in the Magician is that of action, purpose and will. He reveals to the Fool his potentials and possibilities; he lays before him a map of personality in terms of elements, and reminds him of the duality of his nature, mortal and divine. In alchemy, Hermes was said to preside over the whole alchemical work; in the Fool's journey he acts as the initiator and guide who will accompany him, unseen, on his way.

In a spread of cards, The Magician indicates an important beginning. This card suggests a time of action, creative initiative, skill and potential in abundance. The equipment needed is available but steps may not yet have been taken towards achievement of the goal. New opportunities for intellectual or creative pursuits are presented, and the possibilities for new ventures seem assured. A great reserve of power and energy is available; it is up to the seeker to decide how it is to be used.

· THE EMPRESS ·

THE EMPRESS

I t is now time for the Fool to move on and meet his earthly mother, the Empress. This card depicts a beautiful, serene woman with long fair hair that is like the golden fields of corn surrounding her. Beyond the rich fields can be seen a forest and waterfall. At her feet the horn of plenty overflows with fruit symbolizing the earth's bounty. A few poppies grow in the cornfields.

The Empress is a symbol of fertility and abundance. Her full robes hint at pregnancy, suggesting potential fulfilled; they are decorated with pomegranates and hemmed with leafy evergreen boughs symbolizing the permanence of life. The many-seeded pomegranates signify conjugal love and fertility while the sheaf of corn on the Empress's lap character- izes the earth's fruitfulness. She wears a necklace of ten pearls, which symbolizes the ten planets that comprise our solar system. The twelve stars in her crown represent the twelve months of the year, the twelve signs of the zodiac and the infinite becoming finite in the twelve hours of day and night. The Empress is seated in a field of ripe corn signifying the natural cycles of the year; time for seed, blossom, fruit and decay. The poppies are the flowers of death, which is ever present, even in the full- ness of life. In the distance, the mature trees stand as an image of the earth's continuity and age, while the water falling into a pool symbolizes the union of male and female combining to produce new life. Everything about the imagery of this card points to natural growth.

The Empress has much in common with Demeter, the Greek version of Mother Nature. She was the goddess of the earth, the mistress of mother- hood, and all young defenceless creatures were believed to be under her benevolent protection. The fruits of the earth, plants, flowers and crops all came under her patronage. As goddess of the fertile soil, Demeter blessed relationships, as well as the fruitfulness of marriage. She was a mother herself, and her only daughter Persephone was very dear to Demeter's heart. Together they tended the earth; side by side they pro- vided man with all the food and shelter he needed to live. However, when Persephone reached adolescence, she wandered off alone to pick flowers, catching the lustful eye of Hades, Lord of the Underworld. He abducted her and took her away with him to be queen of his gloomy kingdom. Demeter so was distraught by her daughter's disappearance that she forsook her duties as earth goddess and declared she would not resume them until Persephone was returned to her. Gradually the crops died, the flowers faded, the earth became barren and the men and women went hungry. All their entreaties fell on deaf ears; Demeter refused to do anything until Persephone came home, even though it pained her to see the children and baby animals die of starvation. Finally, with the assis- tance of diplomatic Hermes, a bargain was struck between Demeter and

Hades. As Persephone had eaten six pomegranate seeds while in the underworld, she was bound to stay there with Hades for six months of the year. The other six months were spent with her mother so, in spring, when Persephone came to spend her time on earth, Demeter and the earth rejoiced and bore fruit. In the autumn, when Persephone returned to the underworld, Demeter mourned and the earth was barren.

Demeter, like many mothers, had difficulty letting go of her child, so she is not only the mother who nurtures, she is also the mother who mourns. When any creations, be they children or other creative works, reach their prime, they must live their own life and the mother-creator must let them go. The Empress can be linked with the full moon, which, on reaching its shining bright potential, must slowly fade into darkness.

The Empress represents the Fool's earthly mother. From her he learns about nature, its rhythms and cycles of growth, death and rebirth, and gains knowledge about the same cycles operating within all humans. He learns about women and their needs and ways, and also learns to care and nurture himself. The Empress teaches him to attend to and respect his own bodily needs. He is loved and cherished by the Empress and is thus able to love and cherish others. Attached as the Fool may be to his Empress-mother, he must also learn to leave her and make his own way in the world if he is to reach his own potential.

In a reading, The Empress represents happy, stable relationships, growth and fertility. This card is a symbol of potential fulfilled and stands for love, marriage and motherhood. The Empress may also stand for all manner of creative pursuits whether it be writing, painting, baking a cake or planting a garden. She symbolizes the satisfaction that may be found from nurturing something to fruition, as well as the pain of its loss.

If the Empress is the Fool's mother, then who else but the Emperor could be his father? Leaving behind the natural feminine softness of the Empress, the Fool comes upon the Emperor, who complements her absolutely by portraying the opposite characteristics.

The Emperor is a mature man who is seated on an impressive gold-carved throne decorated with the heads of eagles. The throne is angled towards the right, the side of action. The powerful eagle is a royal bird that is able to fly higher than any other, with the keenest eyesight of all.

Next to the throne stands a shield with an eagle engraved upon it, symbolizing the spirit encased in matter. The Emperor holds an orb and sceptre as images of worldly power. He wears a gold crown, a symbol of status and authority. The orb he holds in his left hand, the side of creativity, and it represents his rational understanding of the laws necessary for men to abide by. The sceptre is held in the right hand, the side of action; it is a symbol of his masculine creativity and potency. The Emperor's robes are red and purple, colours of power and majesty. Behind him the landscape is barren, in contrast to the lush fertile surroundings of the Empress, symbolizing the sterility of a masculine world founded entirely on authority and discipline. Whereas the Empress reclines comfortably on soft cushions, the Emperor sits bolt upright on his hard throne, ready for action. The image of the Emperor conjures up an impression of power, influence, wealth and status.

The Emperor can be associated with Zeus, the supreme father-god of the Greeks. Zeus overthrew his father Cronus, who swallowed his children at birth to prevent any of them taking his place as ruler of the Golden Age. Eventually Zeus' mother Rhea tired of producing children for her husband to devour, so when Zeus was born she hid him away and gave Cronus a stone wrapped in baby clothes, which he undiscerningly swallowed. On reaching manhood, disguised as a cupbearer, Zeus gave Cronus a potion to drink that caused him to vomit, bringing up all Zeus' siblings. Together they fought Cronus and his brothers the Titans, and when at last Zeus' team won, he divided up the rulership of the heavens, oceans and underworld between them. Although he remained in the position of All-Father, and as such demanded respect and obedience, he was also capable of kindness and compassion. He was the protector of the weak and vulnerable and, as we have seen, having fathered Dionysus he took great care to ensure his son's safe birth, despite all opposition. Zeus dispensed good and evil according to the laws that he established. He was also known as the god of the hearth, and of friendship and the protector of all men.

As the Empress is the mother, so the Emperor is the father, the giver of life, the owner who sows the divine seed. The Emperor's task is to teach the Fool how to handle the material side of life, how to live in, and deal with, the world of men. He instructs him on matters of authority and administration as well as giving guidelines on moral and ethical behaviour. The wisdom the Emperor imparts is of a worldly nature, but is nonetheless essential to the Fool's development. The Emperor is symbolic of a dynamic force, energy channelled into making ideas solid and workable. He represents the drive for ambition and power, wealth and fame. His mode of expression is direct, forceful and outgoing, unlike his consort the Empress, whose feminine energy is receptive and nurturing. The Emperor acts; the Empress is acted upon. Together these two parents guide the Fool, showing him that an excess of either too much masculine or too much feminine energy can be damaging. What is needed is a balance, an equation of the two opposites. The Fool needs to internalize the two different images and use them to find harmony within himself. This theme of balance starts with the Fool's earthly parents and follows through most of the cards he will encounter on his journey.

In a reading, The Emperor points to material success and stability. He stands for authority, ambition and worldly gain or achievement. He indicates the kind of energy required to transform ideas into reality. He is a helpful influence if practical changes at home or work need to be made. The Emperor denotes a time to take control of life in a material or concrete sense.

· THE HIGH PRIESTESS ·

THE HIGH PRIESTESS

The Fool now turns his attention from the earthy plane towards more spiritual matters. The time is ripe for him to encounter the mysterious figure of the High Priestess. She represents his spiritual or celestial mother and is depicted seated between two pillars topped with crescent moons. Between the pillars hangs a veil decorated with pomegranates, behind which we catch a glimpse of water. She wears a simple white dress with a crown of daisies around her head. She looks down in quiet contemplation at the narcissi in her lap.

The pillars are black and white, symbolizing duality. The feminine nature contains both positive and negative aspects, creative and destructive, benevolent and malevolent, fruitful and barren. The crescent moons are a symbol of new life, of promise, while the veil of pomegranates, the sacred fruit of Persephone, queen of the underworld, shows the High Priestess' connection with the unconscious world, the realm of the spirit. The pomegranate is the fruit of the dead as well as the fruit of conjugal love – the latter because of its many seeds. The glimpse of water beyond the veil symbolizes the hidden riches that lie concealed in the emotional depths of the unconscious mind. The High Priestess' robe is white to symbolize virginity and the daisies are the flower of innocence. The Narcissus is the flower associated with death and rebirth, as it is one of the first flowers to emerge after winter.

The simple ethereal quality of the High Priestess contrasts with the earthy richness of the Empress; yet together they combine to form the feminine nature in both its spiritual and earthly sense. The combination of the two forms a healthy whole; too much emphasis in either direction leads to imbalance and, as we have seen, the Tarot strives to teach balance and harmony in seeking to achieve integrity of personality.

In mythology, Persephone was Demeter's daughter and, until Hades abducted her to rule his dark kingdom, mother and child tended the earth together. The High Priestess may be connected with the virgin goddess Persephone, queen of the dead. The virgin symbolizes potential yet to be fulfilled, and the High Priestess stands for the treasures of the underworld waiting to be brought to consciousness. During her time in the underworld, Persephone was fed the heart of Dionysus in the form of pomegranate seeds, and gave birth to twice-born Dionysus-Zagreus, the god of light.

The High Priestess can also be connected with Artemis, the virgin goddess of the moon, and with Hecate, witch and enchantress, goddess of magic. Hecate was the goddess of the dark side of the moon and symbolized the bitter, destructive element in the feminine nature. The bitterness is evoked when the natural potential inherent in the virgin remains unfulfilled.

The High Priestess is connected with occult, secret and esoteric matters, and her emphasis is on unseen talent and potential that needs to be brought to light. All life starts in darkness, whether the darkness is of the womb or the soil, and a period of gestation is necessary for the new life to be formed before it is brought to light. A good example is the foetus developing in the secrecy of the womb until the time is ripe for the fully formed baby to be born into light. Creative ideas take the same course; the artist or author nurtures the spark of creation long before the image or idea takes shape in the form of a painting or book. The High Priestess symbolizes the nurturing of spiritual ideas and the knowledge of occult and esoteric matters, as well as enchantment and magic, which can be used for good or evil. The black and white pillars echo the duality in her nature. The High Priestess is subtle and unobtrusive; her secrets are not easily revealed. The key to understanding her mysteries lies in the sea of the unconscious hidden behind the veil. Only by crossing the threshold of consciousness can that which is conceived in the darkness be brought to light.

The divinatory meanings of this card include potential that is waiting to be fulfilled, secrets that are waiting to be revealed, the wisdom that can be gained from occult or esoteric studies and the development of the feminine powers of intuition and insight.

° The Hierophant °

THE HIEROPHANT

I t is time for the Fool to get to know the Hierophant, his heavenly father. The Empress and Emperor together form the pair of earthly parents; the High Priestess and the Hierophant, or High Priest, join as the Fool's celestial ones. Hierophant means one who reveals sacred or holy things. The ancient word for priest was 'pontifex', which means the 'maker of bridges', and the role of priest was to act as a link or bridge between God and man. The priest sacrifices his life in the material world in order to be of spiritual service to mankind, yet he must also renounce the higher order to which he has access in order to be on equal terms with the people he wishes to help.

Like the High Priestess, the Hierophant is portrayed seated between two pillars. Once again, the pillars are symbolic of duality and the balance that needs to be struck between opposites. The Hierophant wears simple white robes, which symbolize purity of spirit. His crown is gold, denoting masculine or solar energy, and it is made up of three tiers, which represent the three states of being: body, mind and spirit. This signifies the Hierophant's understanding of the physical, emotional and mental spheres of the human psyche. Around his neck hangs a chain with crossed keys – the keys of heaven – suggesting the knowledge of good and evil. As one key is gold and the other silver they also represent masculine and feminine as a balanced whole. His hand is raised in blessing with the first and second finger pointing upwards, and the third and fourth fingers folded down on to his palm and held in place by his thumb. This is an expression of 'as above, so below', meaning that what is on earth is a reflection of what is in the heavens. He is intently studying from the open book on his lap, suggesting that he is willing to increase his knowledge from many sources.

Although the Hierophant is a spiritual figure, he is essentially non-denominational; however, his essence can be likened to the wise centaur Chiron, who was half man and half horse. Chiron was the semi-divine and greatly valued teacher of the young Greek princes, instilling into them the spiritual values and respect for divine law, which they would need to learn before tackling the art of rulership or being trained to fight in battle. One day, Chiron's friend Herakles paid him a visit. Unfortunately Herakles had on his back a quiver of arrows poisoned with blood from the deadly Hydra and somehow, by accident, the tip of an arrow pierced Chiron's thigh. The poison was deadly and any human or animal would have died instantly but as Chiron was semi-divine, he could not die. But the wound was in the animal part of him and could not be healed. He was destined to live forever but always in agony. This injury gave him more compassion than ever for those who suffer. He experimented with many herbs in a desperate attempt to heal the wound, and his remarkable discoveries helped many others, but he could never heal himself. The only way he could be released from pain was to change places with Prometheus, the Titan who had angered Zeus by stealing divine fire from the gods to give to man. Zeus had arranged an agonizing torture as punishment for this crime, which would last for eternity unless another god was prepared to give up his immortality to rescue Prometheus from his agonizing fate. Chiron, weary of living with a wound that could never be healed, gave Prometheus his life and gratefully took his place in Hades.

The Hierophant embodies the spiritual face of the masculine principle. He signifies the urge to find ethereal meaning in life; he is the force behind the forming of celestial or religious beliefs and philosophical values within each man. He stands not only for accepted and traditional theology, but also for the need within each man to test out such teachings or beliefs for himself. The Hierophant is the energy behind the desire to find a personal sacred truth. He thus becomes the otherworldly guide and mentor to the Fool but unlike his counterpart, the High Priestess, whose secrets are not readily revealed, the Hierophant is less mysterious and more direct in his teachings.

The divinatory meanings of this card are those of assistance from a wise or helpful person, as well as guidance on spiritual matters and the need to find spiritual meaning in life. The Hierophant represents the urge in man to understand his higher nature. This may be done through study with the help of another person to help explore this realm, perhaps a teacher, mentor, priest or therapist, or it could be done with the aid of formal learning through classes or books.

· THE LOVERS ·

THE LOVERS

Having completed his childhood under the guidance of his tutor the Magician, and his earthly and celestial parents, the Fool is now ready to stand at the first trial of youth, namely love.

The image on The Lovers card shows a young man standing between two women. From a fluffy cloud above flies Eros, pointing his arrow at the young man's heart. One of the women is blonde and young, dressed in white, the colour of purity and innocence. The other woman is older, dark haired and wears a dress of deep pink, the colour of desire and passion. The garden they stand in is filled with roses, the symbol of love. The young man, whose yellow shirt denotes mental energy and blue tunic stands for communication skills, seems confused and in doubt – it is clear that he is trying to decide between the two women. Eros, son of Aphrodite, goddess of love, has two kinds of arrows; the gold-tipped arrows would strike blinding love and desire into the heart of anyone who is struck; the lead-tipped arrow would fill the recipient with hate and fear.

The image of choice that The Lovers card portrays is thought to have derived from the Judgement of Paris. Paris was a mortal shepherd, unaware of his royal heritage, who unwittingly became involved in a dispute between the gods. At a wedding feast, Eris, goddess of discord, threw a golden apple with a note attached stating 'To the fairest' and three great goddesses, Athena, Hera and Aphrodite, all felt they deserved it. Their squabble became so violent that Zeus, wisely not wishing to become involved himself, demanded that Paris should be the judge. Each of the goddesses turned to him, offering him glittering prizes to tempt him and sway his judgement in their favour. Hera offered to make him lord of all Asia; Athena promised that he should be successful in every battle he fought; but Aphrodite, goddess of love and beauty, merely unclasped her magic girdle, which made her quite irresistible. And if that was not enough Paris' heart was pierced by one of Eros' golden arrows and he was smitten with love and desire. He handed Aphrodite the golden apple without question, and in return the smiling goddess promised him the hand of the most beautiful woman on earth. This woman was the legendary beauty, Helen of Troy; however, Aphrodite omitted to mention that Helen was already married to someone else. The terrible Trojan War broke out when Paris tried to claim his prize, demonstrating how choices in love can have dire consequences.

This myth illustrates the dangers and pitfalls that attend all choices, particularly those made in the name of love. The Fool must learn that love is not a simple matter decided by physical attraction, and the considerations made in affairs of the heart are neither easy nor straightforward. The Fool must also come to understand that any choice in love will inevitably bring about many repercussions and complications, just like the ripples caused from a single pebble dropped into a pool.

The Lovers card is not only about decisions in love; it denotes all choices. Choices bring about changes, and whenever a choice is made it changes the status quo irrevocably. The decision you must make when faced with The Lovers card may involve choosing between lovers; between virtue and vice; or between ambition and love. However, the most important point to remember about this card is that the choice you finally decide upon will inevitably have far-reaching consequences, which is why the decision must be looked at from all angles before a conclusion is reached.

In a layout, The Lovers indicates that there is, or will be, a relationship or love affair involving some kind of trial or choice. It is possible that marriage may follow such a choice, or it may be what the old books described as the 'choice between sacred and profane love'. Alternatively, this card can mean a choice must be made that has heartfelt consequences even if it is not about a love affair.

∘ THE CHARIOT ∘

THE CHARIOT

T he Fool, having struggled with love's complexities, is now ready to encounter the next trial of youth - war. The battlefield image of The Chariot stands in contrast to the gentle fertile image of The Lovers. The Lovers card shows a group standing together in a garden of roses, wearing coloured flowing robes, whereas The Chariot depicts a lone figure valiantly struggling to manage two powerful horses as they traverse a dusty arid plane. The warrior wears a red cloak, the colour of passion and aggression, and on his breastplate is the emblem of Scorpio, the zodiacal sign that is co-ruled by Mars, god of war. The horses, one black, the other white, which seem to be pulling in different directions, symbolize the opposing and conflicting sides of human nature: emotion and intellect, weakness and strength, love and hate, cowardice and courage.

The Chariot may be connected with Ares or Mars, the passionate, fiery-tempered god of war who was always involved in one skirmish or another. His method of fighting was to use brute force, and it might indeed have been his masculine strength and pride that attracted Aphrodite, the goddess of love. The warrior and lover are said to walk hand in hand and, in myth, Ares and Aphrodite were lovers. Their union bore a child named Harmonia, or Harmony, symbolizing the positive results of uniting and reconciling opposites.

Another mythic link with the Chariot is that of Phaeton, son of the god Helios who drove the golden chariot holding the sun across the skies to give light and warmth to the world. His teenage son Phaeton wanted to take charge of the chariot but his father warned that he would not be able to control the horses. Determined to have his way, one day Phaeton rose earlier than his father, harnessed the horses to the sun chariot and took off into the skies before his father could stop him. Predictably the young man could not control the horses and the chariot veered far away from the earth, causing parts of it to freeze, while coming dangerously close to other parts, scorching the land and burning the people who lived there. In the end Zeus sent down a thunderbolt to strike down the unfortunate Phaeton and preserve the earth, as it was in imminent danger of destruction. This myth also gave a poetic reason for the climatic changes around the world.

The Chariot describes the conflict that opposites create. In the myth of Phaeton it started with conflict between youth and age. The card depicts the charioteer attempting to control his horses, which represent the opposing aspects of himself, each of which is different and so wants to pull in a different direction. The story of Phaeton warns of what can happen if the horses are not controlled properly. The charioteer must balance his divergent horses to prevent them from pulling too far in one direction, or turning in on one another. The opposite forces may be thought of as the carnal and spiritual forces within man that need to be balanced. They can also represent the wish to go forwards to find new adventure, and the simultaneous desire to be secure in the tried and tested. The Fool, as the charioteer, must learn how to steer a middle course through the battleground of his opposing feelings, thoughts and desires. Although uncomfortable, the confusion brought about by the opposition can be creative, for conflict is necessary to promote change and growth. No change occurs when there is stagnation. Conflict is not something to be shunned, however, because it is an unavoidable part of human nature; rather it is something to be faced with courage, because its resolution can be positive.

In a reading, The Chariot represents the quality of energy needed to fight for a desired goal. It shows a struggle or conflict of interests, and can mean a fight for self-assertion that is necessary. However, if well placed in the spread, a successful outcome is assured, as is triumph over difficulties and obstacles.

The Aces

The Ace or Number One is the beginning of all things. One is the number of creative power and potential. It is the primary number from which all the others grow. All the Aces show a tremendous upsurge of energy; they indicate new beginnings of a vital, positive and vigorous nature.

Ace of Wands

The image on this card shows a strong hand emerging from a cloud, offering a flaming wand. The distance reveals a castle on a hill, which is a promise of what the future might bring. Wands correspond with fire, the element of creativity, energy and initiative, and the Ace suggests positive new beginnings and ideas along such lines. The Aces all stand for energy in its purest form, so the fiery Ace of Wands represents pure creativity. This card could symbolize new understanding, a new business venture, new foundations and creative powers with plenty of potential and ambition to progress and succeed.

Ace of Cups

A hand appears from the clouds, this time bearing a jewel-encrusted cup. Five streams of water brim over the edge and fall into a beautiful lily pond. The streams stand for the fives senses. The water lily is a symbol of emotional growth. The suit of Cups is associated with water, the element that governs feelings and emotions, so the Ace of Cups represents the purest aspect of emotional energy. It can indicate the beginning of a new relationship,

the renewal of strong emotions, love, marriage, motherhood, or the kind of joyful reward that may be gained from a loving union.

Ace *of* Swords

This card depicts the double-edged sword, which cuts both ways, for good and ill. A wreath circles the tip of the sword. It is made up of the olive branch of peace and the palm leaf of victory. The suit of Swords corresponds to the element of air, and to the intellect. It also points to strife and difficulty. The Ace of Swords is a card of strength in adversity, and often indicates that out of evil something good will come. A situation that looks bleak in the beginning can surprise us and turn out to

be extremely promising. A sense of inevitable change comes with this card: 'the old order changeth'. It is a card of great power, force and strength.

Ace *of* Pentacles

This time the hand from the clouds offers a large golden pentacle. A well-tended garden beneath indicates the positive reward for hard work. The Pentacles correspond with the element of earth, the element of the body, matter and material gain. This suit can also stand for worldly status and achievement, as well as for material security or wealth. The Ace of Pentacles signifies strong beginnings for financial propositions, business ventures or enterprises. It can mean the successful

founding of a business that may bring financial rewards, or prosperity and security firmly based. It might also indicate a lump sum of money, or gifts, perhaps of gold.

The Twos

The number Two reveals opposites: positive and negative, male and female, spirit and matter. The pure energy of the Aces is split into opposing forces that can create conflict or balance. The duality of the Twos manifests in the following cards as a balance of forces or a creativity not yet fulfilled.

Two of Wands

As we have seen in the Ace, the Wands signify enterprise, energy and growth. The man depicted on the image stands on the walls of a castle with two wands held firmly in place, symbolizing what he has already achieved. He seems to be considering his future, and trying to decide his next move. The salamander motifs that adorn the castle battlements represent the creative energy of fire, but the essence of the card is potential as yet unfulfilled.

The card denotes high ideals and aims, a desire for travel and a new outlook from the present environment. Change is in the air, and a sense of intuition and vision; initiative can overcome obstacles.

Two of Cups

This card is a good example of the balance of opposites that the Two represents: a man and a woman exchanging cups. The Cups are a symbol of feelings and emotions, the pure energy that overflowed in the Ace. Now the energy is divided; two people are involved and both their interests need to be considered. The serpents of good and evil twine around the pillars as emblems of love's positive and negative attributes, while the carved

lion, usually associated with carnal desire, has the wings of spirit, indicating a happy balance between spiritual and carnal love. This card denotes the beginning of a romance or well-balanced platonic friendship.

Two *of* Swords

A blindfolded woman sits at the water's edge. The blindfold indicates that she can't see her way through the present situation, so she steadfastly ignores her sea of emotions and the jagged rocks of hard fact behind her. Her raised swords are well balanced for the moment, but she is in a precarious situation. This is the card of stalemate; the balanced forces have immobilized each other. The conflict has reached an impasse. The woman seems so frightened, or unsure of which way to turn, that she does nothing. It's as though she hopes that by not confronting the issues they will go away. However, with courage, a change can be made, and good often comes out of what seems to be a bad situation.

Two *of* Pentacles

A young man is happily balancing two pentacles, although behind him the sea is rough. He appears to have a light-hearted, casual attitude. In the distance, the ships, which represent his fortunes, are experiencing some choppy seas but the young man keeps his eyes on the pentacles for the time being. This card stands for the necessity to keep several propositions going at once. The flow of movement, however, indicates that skilful manipulation achieves success. There is change, particularly with regard to financial matters, but also harmony within that change if only the young man can remain flexible enough to allow everything to keep moving.

The Threes

Three is the number of growth and expansion. Number One contains the idea, number Two is the pair who can carry it out and number Three bears the fruit. The three also signifies initial completion, the first stage achieved.

Three *of* Wands

THREE *of* WANDS

The man we saw depicted in the Two of Wands reappears. He has left the safety of the castle and is now looking out over wider horizons. The three wands staked in the ground suggest that he has made his initial decision, but he is now ready to proceed further. The distant pyramids stand for ancient wisdom and the ships represent the imagination. The presence of the salamander indicates the fire connection. Efforts are rewarded in this card and an initial completion is achieved. It is a card of satisfaction and challenge. It could be likened to someone working single-mindedly until a job is finished, only to realize that this is just stage one and that the next phase will follow fast.

Three *of* Cups

Three maidens dance and hold their cups high in joyful celebration. They wear floral garlands around their waists and heads. The pool in the foreground, which has a fish fountain at its centre is a symbol of the water element, suggesting the outpouring of emotion. The image clearly depicts a celebration or joyful occasion. It can signify a marriage or birth, emotional growth, and a feeling of happiness in achievement. It can indicate the

THREE *of* CUPS

conclusion of a happy situation or a healing of wounds. As with all the Threes, however, there is a sense that it is important to enjoy the moment of rejoicing for there is still much hard work ahead.

THREE *of* SWORDS

The Three of Swords shows a stained-glass window depicting a heart pierced with three swords. Storm clouds in shades of blue and grey, the colours of air, indicate stormy weather for the emotions. There may be quarrels or separations as a result; maybe tears over a faithless lover. There is nevertheless a powerful sense of the ground being cleared for something new. Amid the sorrow there is a sense of relief; 'the darkest hour is before the dawn'. This card signifies a flash of understanding or insight into a situation as it really is, which helps to put the sorrow into perspective. This card suggests that the difficulties experienced in relationships can be overcome if faced and worked with honestly.

THREE *of* PENTACLES

This card shows a craftsman leaving a building that has reached the first stages of completion. The discussion could be about ideas for the next phase of work. Three pentacles carved into the staircase show the completed work while scaffolding indicates the unfinished part of the structure. A little mouse scurrying down the stairs connects the card with the element of earth. Once again, the initial completion of work has been achieved and now only the finer details need to be added. As with the other Threes, a sense of achievement can be deservedly enjoyed; however, there is still much to be done.

THE FOURS

The number Four forms a square, with each side equal. It is the number of reality, logic and reason. The essence of man's threefold nature – mind, body and spirit – is brought to the material place, to form a square.

FOUR *of* WANDS

Garlands of fruit and flowers form a canopy supported by four wands, which are firmly rooted in the ground, symbolizing a secure base. A man raises a wreath, a symbol of success, above his head in a gesture of triumph. In the distance stands a castle denoting achievement. Crowds are coming from the castle to welcome their conquering hero. Here we have the solidity of the Four mingled with the energy and enthusiasm characteristic of the Wands; so the result is a happy and productive card. This card indicates the satisfaction of the 'harvest home': celebration and reward after labour, a pause in activities and a tranquil time of rest. It may signify a well-deserved holiday or time of relaxation.

FOUR *of* CUPS

A young man sits cross-legged, arms folded discontentedly, gazing at three cups before him. He ignores or refuses a fourth cup offered by the hand in a cloud. He seems to be caught between reflection and action, for the volatile nature of the feelings signified by the Cups isn't altogether comfortable in the solidity of the number Four. The card is one of divine discontent. The young man has a lot going for him, as symbolized by the

cups, with another being offered in a magical way. But he is too bored, confused or unhappy to see the good around him, or take the opportunities available. He turns his emotions inwards. He needs to look at his life in a fresh, more positive, way, and reassess his position.

Four *of* Swords

The image on this card is of a crypt containing a stone tomb carved with two crossed swords. Two more swords point down to a figure lying on top of the tomb. He is dressed in blue robes, the colour of air, and sleeps on his back, hands clasped on his chest. The image of sorrow from the Three of Swords has moved to the background, as the healing process is now in motion. Although the image looks quite threatening, this card denotes a time of rest or retreat after a struggle: a quiet period for thinking things through, the easing of tension and anxiety. It may suggest a time of convalescence after an illness or an unhappy period.

Four *of* Pentacles

The Four of Pentacles shows a richly dressed man holding on tightly to a pentacle. He is sitting on a trunk decorated with bright gold pentacles, as if he fears being robbed. This is the card of the miser; the need to hold on to possessions or emotions prevents gain. The card couples the strength of purpose of the number Four with the material aspect of the Pentacles. A tiny mouse connects the card with the earthy element. The card's message is, 'Nothing ventured, nothing gained.' The attitude towards money reflects the way the emotions are expressed; there is an underlying sense of anxiety, as if there is fear that freedom of feelings will result in emotional hurt or loss.

The Fives

Five is the number of uncertainty. It carries no constant vibration and may change or shift, though it seems that the five in Tarot signifies more adversity than it does in numerology.

Five *of* Wands

FIVE *of* WANDS

Five young men brandish huge wands in combat; a conflict of interest is aptly portrayed. Although a battle is evident, it is important to note that no blood has been shed, nor do the men seem to be attempting to kill each other. The Wands represent creativity, but here they are crossed, implying that the creative process is blocked. This card suggests a struggle in life and love and indicates petty obstacles and annoyances, or short-term communication problems which, once overcome, can change things for the better. In the short term it seems as if nothing works out quite right in work or play; however, Five is the number of change, so this doesn't last for long.

Five *of* Cups

A figure wearing a black cloak of mourning bends woefully over three overturned cups. He appears not to notice the two full upright cups behind him. The spilled cups represent that which has been lost and the full ones signify what remains intact. On a distant hill stands a castle, symbol of hope and security. The river represents grief, and links the card with the water element. The bridge indicates the way across the river towards hope.

FIVE *of* CUPS

This card suggests there may be regret over past actions, but all is not lost. It may be necessary to turn attentions towards what can be salvaged. There are other alternatives to be explored within the loss.

Five *of* Swords

A man stands victorious in battle, proudly holding up three swords, while two defeated warriors slink away. Their swords lie in front of the victor. who seems invincible. They have no choice but to surrender their weapons to him. This card offers the message, 'Swallow your pride and accept your limitations, then move onwards and upwards.' The Five of Swords carries a warning about both victory and defeat: there is danger in deceit that may contribute to defeat, and danger in the arrogance of success. The birds connect the card with the element air and the thinking function, which means it is necessary to evaluate a situation carefully and acknowledge limitations before proceeding in a new direction.

Five *of* Pentacles

Two beggars shelter outside a church. They don't seem to notice the light in the window above their heads, for they are bowed down in sorrow. This is the reverse of the good fortune so often found in the suit of Pentacles. There may be strain or anxiety over money, a warning that temporary financial difficulties lie ahead. This could be deeper than just a lack of money, for the beggars seem also to have lost spiritual direction, as is symbolized by their inability to gain comfort within the church. The card advises that attention should be paid to detail - financial, emotional or spiritual - and it warns that without due care something important or valuable may be lost.

Exercises for Part One

➤ The Major Arcana ᵒ

Now that you have completed the first section, here is an opportunity to get to know your cards more deeply. This first exercise is all about getting to know the Fool. Extract The Fool card from your pack and study it carefully. Look closely at his clothing, at what he is doing, at the atmosphere of the card and all the other details that strike you. Write down your first reactions and impressions. Now, try to identify with the Fool; put yourself in his position – after all, you too are at the beginning of a journey into the new and exciting world of Tarot. The Fool is about to take a leap off the edge of a precipice into the unknown, strange territory that lies below him. Imagine the feelings and thoughts that might be flashing through his mind, as he stands poised on the edge. Would his feelings be similar to those going through your mind as you start on your journey into the Tarot? You may be nervous, as is the Fool, but like him you stand to gain greater benefit as a result of daring to take up this challenge.

Now think about the following questions and either write down or make a recording of your initial reactions.

How would you describe yourself as you embark on your journey?
What do you hope to gain?
What do you have in common with the Fool?

Now you can tackle a 'guided fantasy' exercise. First, and most importantly, make sure you will not be disturbed. Set aside enough time to be alone and relax fully. Turn the telephone off and make yourself comfortable. Sit or lie down, whichever allows you to relax the most, and take several deep breaths. Relax every muscle in your body as completely as you can. Close your eyes and clear your mind; try to free yourself of the day's events and the week's worries.

When you feel peaceful and at ease, take The Magician card and look at it closely. Keep looking at the picture until you can see in your mind's eye when you close your eyes. Now try to imagine the card surround as a window frame. Visualize yourself climbing through it and standing alongside the Magician. Picture him as a real-life figure. See the soft folds of fabric of his robes; notice the glinting of the gold and metal objects on his table; smell the perfume from the roses and lilies in his garden.

Now imagine that you are holding a conversation with him. Ask him questions and allow him to answer, paying close attention to what he says. Talk for as long as you like, but when you feel ready to bid the Magician farewell, make sure you 'close the fantasy down' properly by climbing back out of the window and imagining the image as a card again. The closing down is an important part of the exercise. When you are ready, open your eyes and write down or record your talk with him. Note your feelings and thoughts about the meeting with care. The more of a personal record you can build up, the better rapport you can expect to have with your cards. It may seem awkward at first, and you may feel foolish, but if you persevere, this exercise of the imagination will conjure up many different thoughts and associations for you personally with each card. It is the best way to get in tune with your pack and with the deeper meaning of the cards.

Now, in your own time, repeat both exercises with all the other Major Arcana cards that we've looked at so far. As with any study, it takes time and effort but it is extremely worthwhile when done properly.

⇒ The Minor Arcana ⇐

Go through all the Minor Arcana cards that we have looked at so far, and try to associate the essence or feeling of each card with something from your personal experience. For instance, does a particular card remind you of the first time you fell in love, had your heart broken, lost your job, moved home? Note whatever comes to mind for you personally, as you study each card and jot down your immediate reaction. The hard work you put in now will reward you richly when you start to conduct readings.

PART TWO

MAJOR CARDS

Justice

Temperance

Strength

The Hermit

The Wheel of Fortune

The Hanged Man

✢

MINOR CARDS

The Sixes

The Sevens

The Eights

The Nines

The Tens

The Next Phase in the Fool's Journey

Now let us continue with the next stage of the Fool's journey. He has received the benefits of his education with his teacher (the Magician), his worldly parents (the Empress and the Emperor) and his celestial parents (the High Priestess and the Hierophant); he has learned lessons in love and war (the Lovers and the Chariot); and is now ready to attend the 'school of life' and face the worldly trials of adulthood, (Justice, Temperance, Strength and Prudence or the Hermit), also known as the four moral lessons of life. Halfway through his life (the Wheel of Fortune) the Fool experiences some form of loss or crisis. This evokes in him a need to sacrifice and change (the Hanged Man).

❧✿❀❦

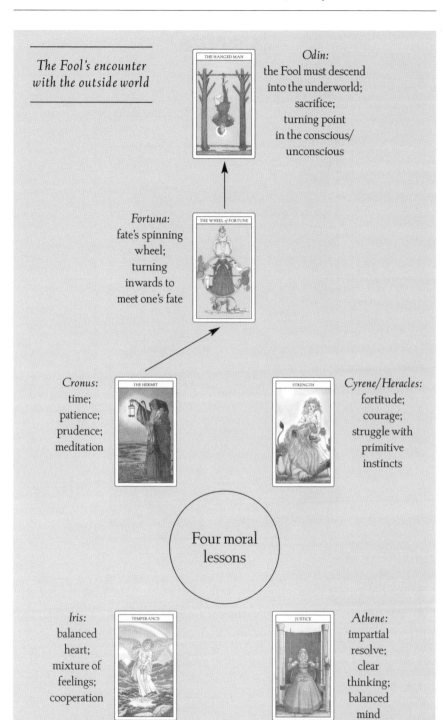

The Fool's encounter with the outside world

Odin:
the Fool must descend
into the underworld;
sacrifice;
turning point
in the conscious/
unconscious

THE HANGED MAN

Fortuna:
fate's spinning
wheel;
turning
inwards to
meet one's fate

THE WHEEL *of* FORTUNE

Cronus:
time;
patience;
prudence;
meditation

THE HERMIT

STRENGTH

Cyrene/Heracles:
fortitude;
courage;
struggle with
primitive
instincts

Four moral
lessons

Iris:
balanced
heart;
mixture of
feelings;
cooperation

TEMPERANCE

JUSTICE

Athene:
impartial
resolve;
clear
thinking;
balanced
mind

The Fool must now attend the 'school of justice', the first of the cardinal virtues. The figure on this card is pictured seated between two pillars wearing a red robe, a green cloak and a yellow headdress. Red is the colour of the planet Mars, the god of war, and green is the colour of the planet Venus, the goddess of love; thus the colours of the figure's clothes combine to symbolize the harmony inherent in the balancing of opposites. The yellow of her headdress signifies thought and communication. The pillars, which are reminiscent of those on The High Priestess and The Hierophant cards, depict the eternal opposites, and the purple veil that hangs between them is the colour of wisdom. On a shorter pillar sits an owl, the bird of wisdom, known for its clear vision and ability to see in the dark. Justice is an imposing figure, staring straight ahead. The sword she holds in her right hand, the hand of action, is masculine and symbolizes the truth, while the scales held in the left hand of creativity are feminine, and stand for balance. The zodiacal sign of Libra, associated with equilibrium and harmony, uses the scales as its symbol. The card of Justice may be connected with the element of air, and the power of the intellect.

The figure on the Justice card may be connected with Athene, the wise goddess of the Greeks. She used the power of the intellect to its fullest capacity and, although essentially a warrior goddess, she preferred to fight battles using the application of intellect and strategy, rather than brute force. This card, in contrast to The Chariot, shows that battles can be won using brain not brawn. Athene was venerated as the goddess of prudent intelligence, and she was a protector of heroes, guiding many on perilous expeditions and providing them with the necessary advice. Those who were prudent enough to listen to, and heed, her wise advice benefited enormously and returned from their quests unscathed.

Myth tells of a contest between Athene and Poseidon, god of the ocean, in which each had to produce an object that would be precious to mankind. As a prize, a great city would be named after the winner. The other gods on Olympus gathered around to judge which gift would ultimately be of most use to the human race. Poseidon stepped forward to make his offering, striking open the ground with his powerful trident. Out sprang the first horse that the gods and men had ever seen. The gods were suitably impressed and began to mutter that they doubted Athene could produce anything that could match such a wonderful creature. And when Athene came forward modestly holding an olive tree, the first of its kind, they looked even more doubtful. However, Athene quietly informed the assembly of the olive's many virtues, pointing out that the fruit and oil would nourish man's body, its wood could be used for fires and shelter, but, most importantly of all, its leaf was an emblem of peace, which man needs far more than war, which the horse symbolizes. In the end, the gods deemed peace to be the most precious gift, so Athene duly won the contest and the city of Athens was named in her honour.

Justice teaches the Fool to discriminate, to make dispassionate evaluations and to make impersonal decisions. At this stage of his journey, he must learn to solve his problems impartially: to weigh up, to balance and then to make rational judgements. Justice is fundamentally a human conception centring on fairness and reason. Nature, however, is not fair, nor is it reasonable, at least according to man's interpretation of the word. Even so, man at his best strives to be fair and to use justice in an attempt to establish equilibrium as a guiding principle of his world and on his society. Although his ideal may seem hopelessly naïve because nature can never be tamed by man, justice is nevertheless one of the most noble conceptions of the human spirit.

In a reading, Justice stands for the need to weigh things up, to find fair and rational solutions, for reason and thought to override emotions, although at times Justice might need to be tempered with mercy, as we will see in the next card, Temperance. In short, it stands for the need for a balanced mind.

◦ TEMPERANCE ◦

The Fool has learned the value of a balanced mind through his encounter with Justice; he now needs to complement this with a balanced heart. He meets the rainbow-winged angel of Temperance, dressed in white robes with a golden triangle contained within a square on his chest. In the sky behind is a shimmering rainbow. The angel pours water from a golden cup into a silver one, and stands with one foot on land, the other in the water. A road leads away from the pool towards twin mountain peaks, between which the sun is rising.

The angel's robes are white to express his purity, while the triangle symbolizes the spirit's ability to rise from within the square denoting the physical body. The wings of Temperance hint at his supernatural quality, and he pours the water of feeling from the golden cup, symbolizing consciousness, into the silver one, which stands for the unconscious, thus showing the need for a constant flow between the two. If water doesn't flow, it stagnates, as do feelings if they don't exchange through communication. Gold is the metal of the sun, and is therefore connected with the masculine principle, while silver is the metal of the moon and the feminine, thus the flow of water between the two signifies the mixing and blending of the opposites. The placement of the angel's feet echoes this, as earth and water are associated with the conscious and unconscious respectively. The road leading to the mountains represents both balance between opposites and a route for the Fool to follow. The rising sun offers new hope in the task of resolving opposites, which are represented by the twin peaks. The rainbow in the sky reflects in the angel's wings as a symbol of promise and hope, expressed in folklore as the 'pot of gold at the end of the rainbow' or in children's songs as a land beyond the rainbow where dreams come true.

In Greek myth, Iris was the messenger goddess of the rainbow, who served both Zeus and Hera. The rainbow acts as a bridge between heaven and earth, which Iris used to reach earth from Olympus. She was equally at ease on earth, in the sky or even in the depth of Hades, where she would cheerfully descend to carry messages. It was said that the usually unfriendly underworld would open up at her feet when she arrived, sent by Zeus, to fill her cup at the waters of the River Styx, from which the immortals drank to preserve their immortality. Iris was a kind and compassionate goddess whose gentle willingness to help everyone made her beloved of gods and men alike.

The word 'temperance' means moderation and a lack of extremes. Temperance is one of the cardinal virtues, and the pouring from one cup to another may be seen to depict the custom of mixing water with wine to moderate the effect of the alcohol. It may also allude to the Christian communion ceremony during which water is mixed with wine; the water of man is mixed with the blood of Christ, which he shed to redeem mankind.

The Fool needs to learn from Temperance how to mix, in their due proportions, the opposites of success and failure, growth and decay, joy and sorrow; the waters poured by the angel from one cup to the other represent these different feelings and emotions. The care with which the liquid is poured shows the benefit of moderation. Justice may need to be tempered with mercy, and Temperance offers the qualities of compassion and forgiveness and takes into account the feelings in situations rather than just the factual circumstances, as Justice may be inclined to do. The angel of Temperance strives for a sense of emotional calm and serenity, the feeling equivalent of what the mind knows as Justice.

In a reading, Temperance stands for the need for cooperation in friendships and partnerships. It signifies successful marriages and relationships because of the compromise that is required in the blending together of opposites. The Temperance card denotes the need for a balanced heart.

· Strength ·

STRENGTH

T he Fool has gained experience in thought and feeling; now he must develop the capacity to control, discipline and weigh up these elements within himself. He learns these lessons through the card of Strength, which shows a woman holding open the jaws of a lion. Some Tarot cards depict Strength as a struggle between a man and a lion, although in Renaissance art the virtues were often portrayed as female, sometimes dressed ready for the battle against vice.

The card depicts a beautiful maiden in a flowing white robe, her hair adorned with a wreath of roses and lilies, while garlands entwine her waist. Although she is standing in a peaceful green meadow, appearing the very picture of femininity, incongruously she is holding open the jaws of an enormous lion. Once again, this imagery shows the blend and union of opposites; the maiden, whose white dress represents the moon and femininity, and the lion, a solar animal, symbolizing the sun and masculinity. The card also alludes to alchemical imagery, with the powerful lion representing the masculine, fiery, active principle of Philosophic Sulphur uniting with the graceful maiden who represents the feminine, watery, passive principle of Philosophic Mercury. The union between these elements can transform into the higher elements of gold and silver. The combination of red roses and white lilies represents the masculine and feminine in a harmonious blend. The maiden is not trying to kill the lion; she is trying to tame him, and the lion, symbol of strength and power, is submitting to her will. There is no evidence of brutal force, only an impression of a firm command, which the lion obeys.

Greek myth tells of a time when Apollo, the sun god, encountered Cyrene, a hand-maiden to the moon goddess Artemis, struggling bare-handed with a fierce lion. Cyrene won her fight, and Apollo was so charmed with her courage and fortitude, as well as her feminine beauty, that he spirited her off to a paradise land where she enjoyed harmony and peace ever afterwards. Some myths say he took her to Libya, where he had a city named after her. Some decks show the image of Heracles struggling with the Nemean lion, which he tried in vain to kill with swords and arrows. He finally resorted to a bare-handed fight and succeeded in strangling the beast. He kept the lion's skin, however, and wore it as a cloak of protection, which rendered him invulnerable. A great many fairy tales and myths tell of a hero's journey or quest that involves a meeting with a wild animal who is helpful, but who must first be tamed by the hero before it can become a travelling companion.

These myths are useful when looking at the psychological lessons this card offers. The lion stands for instinctive desires and wishes, which, although they should not be denied or repressed, sometimes need to be controlled. A child doesn't have this sense of self-control from birth; it is something that is acquired during the development of the personality. A child needs to learn that it's not always appropriate to do as we please, and we must therefore, acquire some self-discipline. This is not the same as denying the impulse altogether. Heracles struggles with the lion and kills it, but then wears its skin as protection. The beast within must be acknowledged and integrated for it to be of use. This card represents the strength and endurance necessary to achieve self-control. It suggests that obstacles can be overcome through willpower, resulting in a sense of mastery. Leo is the zodiacal sign that represents individuality and self-mastery, and uses the lion as its emblem.

In a reading, this card shows courage, strength and determination. It offers the possibility of achieving self-awareness and conviction. One of its chief messages is the need for discipline and self-control. It represents the potential of integration and individuation.

· THE HERMIT ·

THE HERMIT

After the colour and vibrancy of the previous cards, the Fool comes upon the grey stillness of the Hermit. Although this card displays the most lacklustre colours of any of the Major Arcana the Fool has encountered thus far, this doesn't mean it is dull or symbolic of stagnation.

The image is of an old man whose head is bowed down, shrouded in a grey hooded cloak. Only his hands and a tiny portion of his face are exposed. He has a long white beard and holds a staff in his left hand. He is a mysterious figure, standing alone against a grey horizon. Even the earth's natural richness seems to have deserted him; all that can be seen of the landscape is a stony path and parched grey earth. At the man's feet is a small brown snake that accompanies him on his journey. The only thing that offers him light and warmth is his lantern, which he holds in his right hand and which emanates a warm, golden glow.

The Hermit's white beard symbolizes age and maturity; he looks down carefully to see where he is going, an action that suggests wisdom and experience. Unlike the Fool, who doesn't look where he is going as he walks off the cliff, the Hermit is clearly concerned about his progress; he keeps his eyes lowered and holds out his lantern to light his way, using his staff for support. The snake is a symbol of transformation as it sheds its skin of youth and grows a new one in old age. His lantern denotes the light he uses to illuminate his inner world, which, as he grows older, he learns to appreciate.

This card can be connected in Greek myth with Cronus. Cronus, or Saturn to the Romans, was the god who ruled the Golden Age of Man. He dreaded losing his power and did not want to give up his rulership of this special time. He had been warned by an oracle that he would be overthrown by his children, so in an attempt to prevent this he swallowed each of his offspring at birth. Eventually, his wife Rhea, utterly exasperated at producing children for her husband to dispose of in this unfriendly manner, tricked Cronus into swallowing a stone wrapped in swaddling clothes. The real baby boy, Zeus, was hidden away and grew to manhood in secrecy. On reaching adulthood, he appeared to his father disguised as a cup-bearer and gave him a potion to drink that caused Cronus to vomit, bringing up his swallowed children. They then helped their brother and redeemer wage a war against their murderous father and finally overthrew him as had been foreseen. Zeus banished Cronus to live in the Isles of the Blessed, where he ruled peacefully as the god of time and old age. The Latin version of the story ends by adding that, if Cronus waits patiently enough, the Golden Age will one day return.

The image of The Hermit, with its starkness and lack of detailed imagery, comes as a surprise after the vibrancy of the previous cards. However, the card clearly indicates that the time is ripe for withdrawal from the busy outside world in order to enter the quiet inner one. This means freeing our minds of the external hurly-burly to allow time and space for our thoughts to clear. The Hermit teaches the lesson of time, and the inevitability of old age. Time and change must be accepted as part of the natural cycles by which man lives, for they involve constant flow from birth to blossom to fruit, and the return of the seed back to the ground. Although we may all wish to halt the ageing process, the Cronus myth tells us that no matter how hard we try we cannot succeed; time will eventually claim us all.

Another of the sobering lessons the Hermit has to teach is that of solitude, one of man's greatest fears. The truth is that we are all always alone, but to face this fact is often uncomfortable and even frightening. At the same time, however, by facing the truth we are well on the way to accepting it, and once it is really accepted it stops being so frightening. Cronus did not wish to grow old and refused to accept his limitations, but eventually, during his enforced solitary exile, he found inner peace and became content to let time take its course, serenely waiting for the Golden Age to return. Acceptance, patience and inner understanding are the messages learned by the Fool through his encounter with the wise Hermit.

In a reading, The Hermit represents a time for soul searching and meditation, the need for patience and an opportunity to work things out quietly. A degree of solitude is often required and sought, and a wish for temporary withdrawal is permitted.

THE WHEEL *of* FORTUNE

The Fool now reaches the turning point in his journey. He is at the point where he realizes that there is more to life, and to himself, than the external world of relationship, career and status. He glimpsed this during his time with the Hermit, and now, as the Wheel of Fortune turns, he realizes that there is a whole new world beneath the surface that he has not yet visited.

The image on the card shows a blindfolded woman turning a wheel, at the compass points of which are four figures. The woman wears purple, the colour of wisdom, but her blindfold shows that her actions are unpredictable. The four points stand for the four elements of fire, water, air and earth and the four cardinal signs of the zodiac, Aries, Cancer, Libra and Capricorn respectively. Each of the figures attached to the wheel represent a different position; an eager young man looks up as he is on the rise saying, 'I will rule.' In his eagerness to rise to the top he does not look back to see where he has come from. At the top of the wheel a crowned king sits in a position of power and might saying, 'I rule.' From where he sits he doesn't see the falling man beside him. This man is anxious. As he descends he says, 'I have ruled,' but he only sees ahead the beggar beneath him. The figure at the bottom wears rags and has no shoes. He says, 'I am without rule,' and looks at the ground.

The goddess Fortuna was, in Roman mythology, the personification of luck; however, when represented as veiled or blindfolded, she denoted the capriciousness of life. Her Greek equivalent was Tyche, the presiding deity that governed the prosperity of a city and its fate or destiny. Destiny was thought to be an irresistible power that determined the future, based on the idea that there is a natural order or pattern to the universe.

The blindfolded woman symbolizes the goddess Fortuna who turns the wheel of fate and, according to her random turns, man's fortunes rise and fall. The figures on the wheel represent the rising towards success, the achieving it, the losing it and the state of being without any success at all, which again is a reflection of the cycle of life: blossom, fruition, decay and death. This is further echoed by the phases of the moon: waxing, full, waning and old.

Although in medieval times it was fashionable to blame the goddess Fortuna for everything that went wrong in life, these days we tend to own our lives in a more conscious and responsible way. The Wheel of Fortune is a paradoxical image of stability and change. The true self of a man, which is hidden from his conscious mind, very often remains at the still hub of the wheel, like the blind goddess. The hub remains stable, although the external or conscious situations change, as reflected by the moving outer rim. Fate is the circumference of the wheel, and the true self is the centre. The hub enables the rim to turn and thus controls all that comes its way. Each man is responsible for his own destiny, and although circumstances are determined, as are the four points of the great wheel, it is each man who turns his own wheel to whichever point his true self dictates. Fate does not seek you out. So, when joy or sorrow comes into your life, it isn't that happiness or misfortune has befallen you, but rather that you have turned to face it. Often, the fear of taking such a responsibility upon our own shoulders causes us to blame fate for the course our lives take. In reality, we are presented with choices and situations, and what we do with them is on our own account. This is the difficult lesson the Fool learns from the Wheel of Fortune, and he must now take responsibility for his own life and fate.

When The Wheel of Fortune appears in a spread, it signifies that a new chapter is starting, a decision of importance is to be made, or that a new run of luck is commencing. The more you are aware of your own power over your destiny, the clearer things will appear.

° THE HANGED MAN °

At this point, the Fool starts his descent into the underworld to explore the realms of his unconscious mind. He confronts a strange figure suspended from a rod that is supported by two trees with six sawn-off branches apiece. He is hanging from one leg, with the other leg tucked behind to form an inverted triangle. He wears a green shirt, and one of his stockings is red and the other one white. A pool lies beneath him, and despite his perilous position, his face is calm; a halo glows around his head.

The inverted triangle is an image of the descent of higher to lower, and the twelve branch stumps represent the twelve signs of the zodiac, suggesting that the sun has run its course through the seasons of the year and is ready to enter the last phase. The man hangs from his ankle, the part of the body attributed to Pisces, the last sign of the zodiac, and the sign of purification and sacrifice. The halo symbolizes the light that must shine in the darkness of the underworld. The Hanged Man's green shirt is a symbol of healing, and his red and white stockings denote passion and purity in equal measures. His hands are firmly held behind his back, showing that he is in no position to move.

The essential meaning of this card is one of sacrifice: the voluntary surrendering of something in order to gain something of great value. In Greek myth, Prometheus the Titan created mankind but suffered dreadful torture in punishment for stealing fire to give to his beloved creations. Prometheus' punishment was dire: he was stretched on an icy mountain-side where an eagle ate his liver by day, only to have it grow back again each night. Prometheus sacrificed himself so that man could share in divine fire.

In Teutonic myth, the god Odin volunteered his own sacrifice and rejuvenation. 'For nine nights,' he says in an old poem, 'wounded by my own spear, consecrated to Odin, myself to myself, I remained hanging from the tree, shaken by the wind, from the mighty tree whose roots men know not.' The tree mentioned was the ash Yggdrasil, the world tree, and by wounding himself and hanging from its branches, Odin performed a magical rite for the purpose of rebirth and rejuvenation. As he hung for those nine lonely days and nights, he waited in vain for someone to bring him food or drink. However, as he hung he looked about carefully at what lay beneath him and noticed some runes – characters carved on stone, which have magical meanings and powers. He managed, with some considerable effort, to pick one up and was immediately released from the tree by its magic. He was filled anew with youth and vigour, and so his resurrection and rejuvenation was accomplished.

The Fool has reached the point in his journey at which knowledge of what lies within him becomes as important as, if not more so than, that

which exists outside. This card represents the turning point in psychological development, the point at which the individual must come to
grips with the unconscious forces within him. He needs to sacrifice control of his conscious ego by surrendering to the unknown territory of his
inner world. It seems that this can only be done by conscious choice; it
cannot be inflicted by others or by the outside world, although external
circumstances may contribute to the Fool wanting to look within. As
Jung says, it is as if the conscious mind volunteers to die in order to bear
a new and fruitful life in the unconscious. Jung points out that there is
always an inevitable fear that arises whenever the notion of taking a trip
to Hades is contemplated. The Fool started his journey with a sense of
trust and willingness to take a risk no matter what, and now, once again,
he must take a risk and dare to make that inner journey.

In a reading, The Hanged Man indicates a time of greater under-
standing. It also suggests that a sacrifice will have to be made,
although it is worth remembering that this action will be taken in
order to gain something of more value.

The Sixes

Six is the number of equilibrium and harmony. The six-pointed star is made of two triangles: one points up towards the spirit or heavens; the other points down towards the body or earth. This symbolizes balance between them.

Six of Wands

A man on horseback is crowned with a laurel wreath symbolizing success and triumph. Another wreath is attached to his wand and a crowd follow him in admiration, applauding and congratulating him. This card is one of achievement, fulfilment of hopes and wishes in one's career, and a sense of great satisfaction. Acclaim is received from others, and public recognition awarded for success. It can mean promotion after good work, or reward for effort expended in a good cause.

Six of Cups

An old dwarf and a little girl are busy arranging flowers in six cups. The child is a symbol of the future, and the dwarf signifies the past, yet they work together in the present. They put the flowers, which represent memories, into the cups, denoting feelings. Behind the pair stands a thatched cottage with a quaint garden and old-fashioned wishing well, conveying nostalgic thoughts of home, family and childhood memories. The Six of Cups can indicate a meeting with an old friend or childhood

acquaintance; an old lover may reappear or a love affair may be revived. Something with roots in the past may be reconsidered, and past efforts may bring present or future rewards. In some circumstances, this card could mean that the seeker lives too much in the past, or is too nostalgic and doesn't pay enough attention to present and future potentials.

Six of Swords

This card presents an interesting combination of the harmony of the Six and the Swords, which so often represent difficulty. A ferryman carries two people across the water to a distant shore. It is interesting to note that the water on the right-hand side of the boat is rough; whereas on the left it is calm. This indicates a move away from difficulties towards more peaceful times. It can mean a literal journey, a move to a more pleasing environment; but it could also be a journey of an internal nature.

This card can denote release of tension and anxiety after a period of strain, so that a sense of harmony may prevail once again.

Six of Pentacles

The number of harmony is shown in this card by a merchant carefully weighing out gold to distribute his bounty fairly among the needy. He uses a set of scales to ensure a just distribution of alms to the poor. The number Six and the suit of Pentacles combine to produce material benefit. This is a card that suggests that money owing will be paid, or that the seeker will receive what is rightfully theirs. There may be financial help from a generous friend or employer, so that material affairs may be put on a stable footing. There is also the suggestion that if the seeker's position is prosperous he should share his fortune with others, as his turn to receive will come around soon enough.

THE SEVENS

Seven is the number of wisdom and relates to the completion of cycles.
There are seven personal planets in astrology, seven virtues, seven vices
and seven deadly sins. On the seventh day, the Bible tells us, God rested.
Inherent in this number is a sense of completion of a phase.

SEVEN OF WANDS

Six wands rise up to attack a young man, who fights bravely. One attribute of the Seven is deep purpose and valour, both of which are aptly depicted here. The figure endures an internal battle with his own creative forces. He wears no boots or cloak, for such protection won't help in the battle of ideas. This card may suggest a successful change in profession. There could be stiff competition in business, but perseverance and courage will win in the end. Strength and determination are needed to achieve goals, and are available if sought. The card also signifies knowledge and includes skills in teaching, lecturing and writing.

SEVEN OF CUPS

Fantastic visions arise out of seven cups floating in the clouds above a daydreaming figure: the castle of security, the snake for sexuality, the dragon representing strength, the jewels signifying wealth, the laurel wreath of success, the dove of the spirit or the draped figure representing the true self. He doesn't seem to know what to choose, but a careful, considered decision must be made; otherwise his dreams and ideas will remain 'cas-

tles in the clouds'. This is a phase when the imagination works overtime and choices seem innumerable; to choose one direction seems impossible. But without a decision, nothing will be achieved. Accompanying the confusion is an abundance of creative and artistic talent and energy.

Seven of Swords

A man makes a sly escape from a military camp, smuggling out a bundle of swords. He appears to be leaving unnoticed and his expression is one of quiet confidence. This card denotes the necessity for prudence and evasion in order to gain an objective. The number Seven for completion of a phase combines with the airy Swords and suggests that diplomacy and charm are needed in this situation, rather than direct or aggressive tactics. A deed may have been done in secret, and exposure or candid explanations could be dangerous. At its worst, this card indicates a flight from a dishonest act; at best it means 'discretion is the better part of valour'.

Seven of Pentacles

A young farmer stands between two fields. One is established and cultivated and contains six pentacles that stand for the fruits of past labour; the other is uncultivated and above it hovers a single pentacle representing future potentials. The completion of a cycle indicated by the Seven means that there could be a pause during the development of an enterprise or business; the young man appears to be assessing what he has achieved, and what will need to be done in the next phase. There may be a choice between devoting energy to the tried and tested, and investing in something less secure but possibly more exciting.

THE EIGHTS

Eight is the number of regeneration and balance of opposing forces. It suggests the death of the old, evil or wrong and makes way for the new, pure and just. The number Eight is the wise shedding of old concepts, habits and ways of thinking as they become inappropriate.

EIGHT OF WANDS

A figure shoots eight wands from a huge bow and they fly freely through the sky. Their flight in so many directions indicates the numerous possibilities available. The Wands signify creativity and imagination, and the castle on the hill suggests a goal. The salamander is a reminder of the fiery nature of the Wands. Eight is the number of regeneration and, combined with the Wands, denotes a time for activity and new beginnings. It marks the end of a period of delay or stagnation, and indicates a time for initiative and action. This is a busy and exciting time, when life runs according to plan. There may be travel and interesting career moves.

EIGHT OF CUPS

A man walks through an arch of full, neatly stacked cups. He heads for a barren mountain without looking back. The care with which he has collected and arranged the cups shows his previous concern, but now he is ready to discard them. The waning moon symbolizes the end of a phase. It is time to leave the past behind through disappointment or disillusion. While much has been invested in a situation or relationship, it isn't right, so the

seeker must abandon it and search for what is. Although the image is sombre, it marks a necessary transition towards a new life, as is appropriate with the combination of the number Eight and the suit of Cups.

EIGHT OF SWORDS

A woman stands bound and blindfolded in what appears to be a marsh. Eight swords surround her to form a barrier, and behind in the distance stands a castle built on bare rocks. This rather dismal-looking card shows a situation that binds and restricts, yet the constraints result from the figure's own fear and indecision. Although she is bound, her hands are only loosely tied and she could easily free herself if she dared. The swords act as a prison but there is plenty of space to move between them if she could build up the courage. This card suggests that although there are problems to be overcome and important decisions to take, a sign will come to show the way. The paralysis will not last forever.

EIGHT OF PENTACLES

An apprentice craftsman carves out pentacles on his work bench. He seems happy and enthusiastic about his work, the fruits of which are proudly displayed behind him. A mouse, symbol of the earth element, hides under the table. This is known as the 'talent' card, which, when allied with the energy of the number Eight, can indicate the possibility of turning a talent into a profession, or money earned through such a skill. There is possible employment in a skilled field although matters are in the early stages. Hard work and practical ideas form the stable basis for establishing a new and profitable career both in emotional and financial terms.

THE NINES

*In the number Nine, all the power of the lower numbers is combined,
so that together they form a foundation for the ultimate completion
in the number Ten.*

NINE OF WANDS

The Nine of Wands shows strength in reserve.
The fighting figure has a bandage around his head,
which symbolizes an injury, perhaps to his creative ideas as this is the suit of Wands, yet he fights
on. He is ready to defend that which he holds dear,
and the passion he feels encourages him to persevere. The Nine reinforces the power of the fiery
Wands in a bid not to give up in hard times. This
card denotes power and determination and suggests that even if you feel defeated, there is still
enough strength to pull through to the end. It also represents endurance
and resolve, and suggests victory through courage and fortitude.

NINE OF CUPS

The Nine of Cups signifies a state of emotional
and physical bliss. A couple embrace beside a
table laden with fine food and drink. In the distance a fountain represents the overflowing of
emotion. The scene suggests pleasure on all sen-
sual levels; material needs are well provided for, as
is symbolized by the opulent surroundings, and
the loving couple demonstrate that the feelings
are satisfied. The power of the number Nine brings
the emotional suit of Cups to a peak before the final

completion in the Ten. This is known as the 'wish' card, signifying the fulfilment of a desire of paramount importance. It denotes a unique moment, a special time in life that is not part of the mundane or everyday experience.

Nine of Swords

A sleepless woman sits up in bed, her head in her hands, seemingly in despair. Nine swords hang ominously over her head, and butterflies, symbols of the air element, decorate the panel at the bottom of the bed. Her bedspread is decorated with motifs of the astrological air signs Gemini, Libra and Aquarius, interspersed with red hearts, showing a conflict between head and heart. This card suggests that the seeker senses impending doom, but as the swords don't actually touch the woman, these fears may be unfounded. It is possible that although there may be a difficult decision to be made or situation to face, the fear is far worse than the outcome.

Nine of Pentacles

A beautifully dressed woman stands alone in a flourishing vineyard, a symbol of the earth's abundance and generosity. A hunting bird on her gloved hand indicates both her far-reaching intellect and controlled thoughts. A castle in the background denotes material well-being, and suggests that her hard work and perseverance have led her crops to grow and she can now benefit. This card often signifies a solitary pleasure in physical comfort and material success, although this doesn't mean that the person is literally without relationships. It is more suggestive of one who is at peace within and so feels contented without constant companionship. Material benefits are promised and appreciated.

The Tens

*The meaning of the Ten is perfection through completion. The One of
beginning is placed next to the Zero of spirit, so the cycle is then ready to
return to One again. The Ten in the Minor Arcana shows the height of
happiness in the Cups and Pentacles, but trials in the Swords and Wands.*

Ten of Wands

A man is shown carrying an impossibly heavy
burden of ten wands borne in a very awkward
and uncomfortable fashion. The strain seems
almost more than he can bear yet he plods on
towards the town in the distance. This card
denotes a weight that must soon be lifted, or a
problem that is soon to be solved. However, the
oppression is often self-imposed and the seeker
himself could do much in order to relieve his load.
The burden may be physical, mental or emotional
or a combination of all three. However, it is within his power to do something to lighten the strain.

Ten of Cups

A young couple hold each other tenderly as they
watch their two children play contentedly. Behind
them stands a comfortable house, a symbol of stability and security, while the blooming garden
denotes fertility. The distant river is an image of
the constant flow of feelings. This is the ultimate
that the Cups can offer in the way of love; happy
family life is depicted, suggesting lasting contentment in contrast to the ecstasy of the Nine, which

is short-lived. In this card, plenty of love is available to be offered and received. The image conjures up a feeling of gratitude, yet there is a sense that this has been earned through effort rather than luck.

Ten of Swords

A figure lies face down in a desolate marshland. He is pierced in the back by ten swords and appears to be dead. Beyond the calm lake, however, the dawn is breaking. The butterfly hovering over the body is a symbol of resurrection and new life. The card obviously signifies an ending; it could refer to a relationship, job, or particular circumstance, or even a false way of seeing a situation. It has a ring of truth and clarity of vision, which brings about an inevitable death, while the new

dawn heralds the promise of rebirth. This grim-looking card has a positive air; the ground is cleared for something new as the increasing light of the rising sun slowly brings back hope.

Ten of Pentacles

A richly robed elderly gentleman, a grandfather perhaps, is seated in the foreground with a child on his knee. Accompanied by his daughter and his loyal dog, the old man symbolizes traditional family life. His castle and estate look well established and the garden is flourishing, which all denote financial stability and firm foundations. This card suggests property acquired for the founding of new generations, and traditions to be passed down through the family, with a feeling of continuity and security. A

materially settled way of life is indicated, and selling or buying property in favourable circumstances also comes under the influence of this card.

Exercises for Part Two

The Major Arcana

At this stage, to familiarize yourself with the cards you have recently met, I suggest that you continue along the same lines as described in Exercises for Part One (*see pages* 64-5). These tasks are vital for forming the core of your understanding of the Tarot images. Use the 'guided fantasy' exercises outlined previously for studying Justice, Temperance, Strength, The Hermit, The Wheel of Fortune and The Hanged Man. As described before, prepare for your exercise and then take careful note of the associations evoked by each image. Record your feelings, thoughts and discoveries as you continue your journey through the Tarot. Write down, draw or paint how each card strikes you, what you notice in particular, and what impression or feeling you are left with after your encounter with each card. If you wish, find pieces of music to associate with the card or think of scents that evoke each card. For instance, you might associate the smell of freshly cut grass with the summery Empress, or the herb sage with the ageing Hermit. Feel free to play around with such associations. This is an opportunity to let your imagination wander!

Pay special attention to the colouring of each card. Do the colours appeal to you? If you are considering colouring your own deck, allow plenty of time to consider which colours work best for you and why. Think about the associations you have with different colours and construct your own colour code. If you are going to design your own colour scheme for your deck, this will be very useful as a starting point.

The Minor Arcana

Using the Minor Arcana cards that you have met in Part Two, think of a description for each card that reminds you of a particular situation or feeling and note which cards stand out most noticeably and why. It is also interesting and revealing to think about why some cards leave you blank. Perhaps you actively dislike them, feel scared or repelled by them; or sometimes, even more puzzling, feel bored or disinterested in them. Rather than just passing those cards over, pay extra attention to them and try to ascertain exactly what it is about them that you find difficult or uncomfortable. Once you have discovered this you will be able to understand them better. We tend to dislike what we cannot understand, so understanding is often a key to liking.

With regard to the colour scheme and symbol code for the Minor cards, take those that you have studied so far and go through each one in turn, searching for clues to the elements and connecting with the colours: reds, yellows and oranges for the fiery Wands; soft blues, pinks and mauves for the watery Cups; ice blues, greys and purples for the airy Swords; greens, golds and browns for the earthy Pentacles. The element clues for the Wands are the salamanders, sunflowers and flames; for the Cups, fish, waterfalls, streams and rivers; for the Swords, clouds, butterflies and birds; for the Pentacles, fruit, foliage and small animals like mice and rabbits. If you are planning to colour your own deck, think about what you would change colourwise, bearing in mind that having one or two colours that reflect each suit uniformly makes it easier to keep the meaning of the element in mind. If you make each card uniquely different, the regularity of the suit may be lost.

PART THREE

MAJOR CARDS

Death

The Devil

The Tower

The Star

The Moon

The Sun

Judgement

The World

MINOR CARDS

The Pages

The Knights

The Queens

The Kings

The Last Phase of the Fool's Journey

The last phase of the Fool's journey brings forth his time in the under-world, following his worldly trials. He has been taught about life in the world through Justice, Temperance, Strength, the Hermit and the Wheel of Fortune – which led him to examine his inner world through his encounters with the Hanged Man. The Fool must age, and through ageing he realizes that there is more to life than worldly matters. In order to find his inner self he must change and transform (Death) and enter the underworld to discover what is at the heart of his inner crisis (the Devil). This involves a struggle with darkness (the Tower), which must be demolished by the light of truth. His search for meaning leads him on to find hope (the Star), endure confusion and doubt (the Moon) and gain optimism (the Sun). His victory over darkness results in rebirth (Judgement) and triumph (the World).

Triumphant achievement

Hermaphroditus:
Success;
attainment;
symbol of goals
achieved;
completion
and reward

St Michael/Hermes:
guides the Fool out
of the underworld
towards success
and rejuvination

JOURNEY TOWARDS THE GOAL

Apollo:
splendour and
triumph;
warmth;
light;
perception
and directness

Artemis/ Demeter/ Hecate:
sleep;
unconscious;
uncertainty;
fluctuation;
change

Star of Isis:
hope; inspiration;
reawakening;
pool of memory
replenished by
star goddess

JOURNEY THROUGH THE UNDERWORLD

House of Hades:
Divine
lightning;
harrowing
of Hell;
reborn of
divine fire

Pan:
purging of
worldly
identifications;
facing own
shadow and
darkness

Hades:
the Fool must
die to be reborn;
stripping of all
pretensions

DEATH

And now the Fool must die. The Death card shows a skeleton on a black horse, carrying a scythe and an hourglass. He wears a white headdress made of the death shroud that was once the swaddling cloth of birth. In the distance a river can be seen with a tiny boat crossing from one bank to another.

Death rides over all people; it is oblivious of rank or position. A king lies outstretched; a bishop holds out his hand as if in prayer; a maiden in a white dress begs for mercy, as if she feels too young, too unprepared to face him. Only the small child appears unperturbed, even holding out a posy in welcome. Children tend not to fear change as much as adults do; they are more accepting of it as so many transitions are made so quickly in early development. We grow more rigid as we grow older.

The scene illustrates the need to face death at some stage, as it comes to us all, no matter how rich, how powerful, how holy, how beautiful or young we may be. Death is unimpressed by worldly status and is not moved by the wealth symbolized by the king, or even the holiness of the bishop. The hourglass signifies the fact that time will run out eventually, as everything on earth has its own time, for life and for death. The scythe is used to gather in a harvest, which Death will do at the appropriate time for each living thing.

The rising sun over the horizon symbolizes a new day and a new life, so welcome after the long dark night of death. The raven pecking at the ground is a harbinger of death, as are the poppies. The river in the background is a symbol of transformation as the water evaporates, turns into cloud and returns to the river as rain. The little boat is an image of both cradle and coffin, for life and death are inseparable. The river may be the Styx, which flows through the underworld filled with the waters of death, but which can also be transformed into the life-giving waters of rebirth and immortality. It could also represent the River Jordan, which Christian souls had to cross to reach the Promised Land.

In myth, the souls of the dead had to cross the Styx river by boat, always being sure to pay a coin to the boatman. If they didn't, they would not make the transition and would remain ghosts, trapped between the living and the dead. Psychologically, the coin represents mourning, which must be properly experienced after a death, in order to allow the mourner to move on after the loss, whatever form it might take.

According to the myth of Dionysus, the jealous Titans tore him limb from limb, threw him into a cauldron and boiled away his flesh, leaving only his skeleton. This, in mythical terms, figuratively represents what happens to the mind and heart of the Fool as he confronts Death. The Hanged Man is the first step towards the Fool's illumination when he consents to surrender his consciousness and makes the journey into

Hades. Death strips him bare of all his pretensions before he is led naked into the presence of the underworld deities.

The Death card symbolizes change, the end of the old and the birth of the new. Life, both human and in nature, consists of constant cycles of death and renewal, as the Fool first learned with the Empress. Each age of man has its phase, and each phase must end when it is lived out. After all, what parents would wish their children not to progress through adolescence into adulthood? It is the natural development, both physically and psychologically, in the life of man. Death simply marks the transition stages. Trees shed their leaves in autumn in order to prepare for the new growth in spring. The skeleton is like the bare tree, stripped of leaves to allow for new spring buds. It represents the falling away of old outgrown feeling and thought under the influence of Death; everything is tried and tested and, if something is found to have outlived its usefulness, it must be discarded. Death can mean the end of things in many different ways. For instance, Death could appear in the spread of someone about to be married, for it would signify the end of their single life, or in the spread of someone about to be divorced, as a symbol of the end of their marriage. Leaving school, leaving home, leaving a job, leaving a country: all these things and more could be indicated by the appearance of Death, but none of these signify a physical death, nor are they necessarily unpleasant. The Death card in the Tarot is connected with transformation and change rather than the death of the body. Feelings, emotions, thoughts and values many undergo a transformation under the influence of Death, as the cycles that govern them end.

In a reading, this card heralds the inevitable ending of something, but with the promise of a new beginning. The pain that is suffered under the effect of Death is related to the willingness or unwillingness of the seeker to surrender to the inevitability of change.

THE DEVIL

THE DEVIL

The Fool's journey is becoming increasingly difficult. His travelling companions are stern, daunting characters, nowhere near as friendly and helpful as the figures he met at the outset of his travels. He has now been stripped of all worldly pretensions by Death, and is led naked and trembling to meet the Devil himself.

The portrayal of the Devil figure is as interesting as it is menacing. The darkness of the top half of the card draws the eye to the black background that enhances the central figure. The Devil, whose torso is half-human, half-goat, sits upon a cube. He has bat wings, horns and a tail, but human hands. He is holding his right hand up, while pointing a blazing torch down to a naked couple below with his left hand. The couple sit in similar positions and are chained by their necks to the block, though their hands are unbound. The man and woman have sprouted little horns and tails, just like the Devil's, which symbolizes that they have allowed themselves to become his disciples. His flaming torch touches their tails to inflame their base desires. Although they are chained to the Devil's cube, which is a symbol of the material world, they could, in fact, lift the chains from their necks to set themselves free. However, they are chained to the Devil by their thoughts as well as by their fear. In order to escape his bondage they must radically alter their thinking; they must think for themselves and not allow greed or lust to overwhelm them. They are slumped in despair and seem too lazy or apathetic to want to change. The Devil has them in his grasp.

The image of the Devil with horns, hooves and tail originates with Pan, the goat-god of untamed nature and sexuality. Hermes fathered Pan with the nymph Droype, but he was born so hairy and ugly that his mother ran away from him in fright. Hermes took him up to Olympus to amuse the other gods, but once they had had their fun mocking him, they banished him to rule the pastures and woods of Arcadia, deeming him too ugly to live with them in beautiful Olympus. He lived happily in Arcadia and was worshipped by the Greeks as a life-giving fertility god, abundant and procreative. He represented natural energy in its chaotic and disordered state. Pan personified the primitive, instinctual urges in man, particularly those of a sexual nature. However, with the advent of Christianity, Pan was banished to hell in the form of the devil as we know him today. Natural impulse and instinct was then frowned upon as evil, and man became ashamed to acknowledge his connections with the physical and sexual side of his nature, as it was associated with the bestial.

The Devil teaches the Fool to recognize and accept all aspects of his nature, both dark and light. He represents the blockage of repressed fears and feelings which, once removed, can release a great deal of positive energy. Energy in itself is neutral; it is how it's channelled that makes it positive or negative. The Devil points out that if neither aspect of our nature is accepted, many inhibitions and phobias can accumulate unconsciously to prevent normal growth and development of the personality. In other words, the 'devil' in each of us must be faced before we can come to terms with him and put his energy to good use.

In Jungian terms, the Devil represents the 'shadow', that part of our psyche we would rather ignore, the tiresome bit we prefer to see in everyone else but never in ourselves. However, if the Fool is able to accept and own his shadow side, he will be more able to feel tolerance and compassion for himself and, in turn, will be able to feel this towards others. Acceptance will take the place of blame, as he begins to understand that all humans are composed of a combination of good and evil, light and shadow, positive and negative, and it is this understanding that enables him to become fully human and accept his human limitations and failings.

In a reading, The Devil's message is that if those blocks and inhibitions that hinder development can be removed, great growth and progress is possible. There is much energy tied up in repression that could be better utilized. 'Out of apparent evil, much good can come.'

THE TOWER

The Fool now faces the lightning-struck Tower, the point at which he must split hell open and release himself from the darkness of the underworld. For the first time on his journey, he encounters a card image that centres on a man-made structure. The card shows a tall building standing in a stormy sea with waves lashing its base. There are three narrow windows at the top from which two figures fall. A man and a woman hurtle down to the raging sea, their faces contorted with fear as they plunge headlong into the unknown. A violent storm is raging;

forked lightning has blown the roof right off, leaving flames in its wake as cracks appear down the sides of the building. It is evidently in danger of imminent collapse.

As a man-made image, the Tower represents the external circumstances that restrict internal development. It is often the society in which we live that governs body, soul and mind, which are symbolized by the three windows. The edifice of the Tower itself represents the social conventions that bind and constrict. The narrowness of the three windows reflects the restrictive nature of the purely material, rational world while the height of their position suggests the possibility of high attainment. The falling man and woman represent unreconciled opposites. The four elements are visible in the imagery: earth – the Tower itself; fire – the lightning; air – the storm clouds; water – the stormy sea. This imagery illustrates the shattering of the Fool's worldly illusions, and the breaking down of false values and beliefs.

Through his encounters with Death and the Devil, the Fool has come to recognize his own inner conflicts, discovering also that he has an infinite number of possibilities at his command. Death has stripped him of his pretensions, the Devil has revealed the extent of his power and now the Tower that encased insincere philosophies must be shattered. The walls of false beliefs and phoney values must be torn down as the divine lightning penetrates the underworld of the unconscious to dispel the dark forces. The fork of lightning is the flash of illumination that splits hell open and breaks down existing forms to make way for the new.

Some Tarot speculators believe that the imagery for this card originates in the biblical story of the Tower of Babel. Babel was the tower that Noah's descendants attempted to construct. They were angry with God for destroying the world by flood and so decided to build a tower so high that they could climb up to heaven and confront the Almighty. Naturally, the plan failed because, in punishment for their supreme arrogance, God commanded that each of the men should speak a different language, which resulted in chaos, and the building of the tower was abandoned.

However, according to Paul Huson, some old French packs use the title La Maison Dieu, which translates as The House of God. Huson suggests that the word 'Dieu' may in fact have been a corruption of the original word, 'Diefel', which means Devil. So, the Tower, far from being the House of God, may actually be the House of the Devil or, in other words, hell. The Fool must escape from hell and the only way he can do this is through the blast of divine enlightenment. This perspective ties in better with the idea of Dionysus being conceived in the darkness of the underworld and born again as Iacchus god of light.

The Tower signifies a time of reckoning; it is the moment that the Fool must sort out for himself what is right for him and abandon whatever is not truly his own. It is often the case that for many years we live as we have been taught, even though what may have suited those who taught us might not actually be right for us. There comes a time when our needs, thoughts and ideas need to be tested, evaluated and ultimately owned. The conflicts inherent in our behaviour when we attempt to structure our lives by convention are symbolized by the Tower, a narrow, constraining structure, while the lightning represents the flash of vision that causes us to change ideas and live our chosen way.

In a layout, this card denotes the necessary breaking down of existing forms to make way for the new. Fresh life and new ways are indicated; rigid or imprisoning structures need to be torn down and replaced. This card stands for the defeat of false values and the triumph of true ones.

THE STAR

THE STAR

At last, the time for renewal is nigh. After the sombre underworld, the shining promise of the Star refreshes and renews the Fool's drooping spirits. Finally he returns to the colourful images like those he encountered when he began his travels. A feeling of release comes upon him as he meets the lovely Star maiden.

A beautiful girl is pouring water from two pitchers, one into the pool as if to replenish it, and the other over the dry earth as if to refresh it. The steady flow of water from the pitcher onto the land divides into five streams. In the background a bird perches in a tree and a butterfly flutters overhead. A large star encircled by seven smaller stars shines softly in the milky dawn sky. The nakedness of the maiden represents truth unveiled; she has no need of protective garments for she has nothing to fear and nothing to hide. She is young; she is a symbol of renewal. The pool she kneels beside might be the Pool of Memory, which, although it was situated in the twilight realm of the underworld, had its waters replenished and refreshed by Mnemosyne, goddess of memory. The Fool may drink from these waters so as not to forget his experience while in the underworld.

The five streams of water stand for the five senses: smell, taste, touch, sound and sight. The bird sitting in the evergreen tree, a symbol of everlasting life, is the ibis of immortality, the sacred bird of Thoth, the Egyptian god of all arts. The bird is a symbol of the soul's ability to rise to high levels of emotional and spiritual consciousness. The butterfly is a symbol of transformation and resurrection. The large central star has connections with the Star of Bethlehem, which heralded new life and hope. The seven stars surrounding it stand for each of the seven ancient planets. Together the stars add up to eight, which is the number of rebirth and of baptism into new and everlasting life.

The Tarot Star has also been connected with the Star of Isis, who was the great mother goddess of Egypt. During the dry season in Egypt, the land became parched and barren. Even the great River Nile, which men relied upon for food and water, would shrink dramatically. The people feared starvation until the longed-for Star of Isis appeared in the skies, heralding the coming of the rains. Then the great river would be replenished and life restored to the dead lands. The people of Egypt rejoiced and were filled with awe and gratitude for the 'magic of Isis'.

Stars have always been an emblem of hope and promise, and seen as a light to steer by. In Greek myth, when Pandora opened the forbidden box, terrible spites flew out and infested the earth. The only thing that did not fly away, but stayed to comfort Pandora in her time of affliction, was Hope. The Three Wise Men followed the bright star to Bethlehem, hoping to find the Messiah; astrologers gain knowledge and insight by charting the movement of the heavenly bodies through the skies, and mariners use the stars to set their ships' courses. Even songs tell us that if we wish upon a star, our dreams will come true.

All men need a goal, an aim towards which to strive. We all need faith, and belief that our hopes and wishes will be fulfilled, that our dreams can come true. Without this hope, our lives lack meaning and eventually we lose the will to continue. The Star is symbolic of our faith, whatever it may be; it does not have to be religious or spiritual in an orthodox way, but if we lack a sense of purpose or a meaning in something, we lose the hope and without that we lose the point in life. Without the inspiration of the Star, life becomes dull and lacklustre. The Star provides that bit of magic that spurs us on and keeps us going in times of stress and doubt. The faith that things can improve is essential when times are difficult, and the image of the Star reflects that inner light which guides us through the darkness.

In a reading, The Star sends a happy message of promise, good fortune, optimism, hope and joy. It suggests inspiration, a sense of purpose and the renewal of life's force and energy. It promises a positive attitude and encourages imagination.

The Moon

As the Fool's journey reaches its final stages, he realizes that there is still much to learn. After the dark sequence of cards in the under-world, he experienced a brief but glorious respite with the Star, only to discover that the next card, The Moon, is another sombre-looking one. At first glance, this card seems similar to The Star, but on closer exami-nation it is not as calm as it appears. The landscape with the pool in the foreground is much like that of The Star; after all, it is still the country of imagination. However, in The Moon card there is no human figure to relate to, only the face of the Moon. A crab crawling out of the pool disturbs its waters, while two animals, a dog and a wolf, appear to be baying at the Moon. A slim winding road leads between twin pillars towards the two mountain peaks in the distance.

The crab, connected to Cancer the astrological sign ruled by the Moon, is symbolic of innermost fears forcing their way to the surface of consciousness. The crab might represent childhood fears reappearing in adult life, still managing to cause fear and anxiety even though we may recognize the lack of logic in this. As the crab crawls up into consciousness, we often try to push him back down in the unconscious. However, if we do this, he nevertheless continues to exist there, still giving rise to vague fears and unacknowledged anxieties until such time as we allow the crab, that is, our fears, to come right out of the pool of the unconscious and be faced. The pool in The Moon has been associated with the Pool of Forgetfulness, which lies to the left of the Pool of Memory in the dark world of Hades. We may want to forget that which gives rises to unpleasant or discomforting feelings or memories, but the crab periodically reminds us of them by struggling out of the water. The other animals in the image, the dog and wolf, are both creatures of the underworld, guides of souls to the land of the dead.

These animals are sacred to Hecate, goddess of the dark moon, enchantment and the infernal regions. Hecate was the triple-headed goddess of the crossroads and was thought to appear when the ebony moon shone. One of her titles was Queen of Ghosts, as she was believed to haunt cemetries. Hovering among the graves, she would prevent harm from leaving, as well as entering, the spirit world. She was often depicted with her two ghostly hounds. Although Hecate was often associated with sorcery and magic, she also did good deeds such as rescuing Persephone from the underworld and restoring her to her mother Demeter each spring.

The idea of dogs and wolves baying at the full moon is a powerful image suggesting madness or lunacy. The road, however, leads between the two pillars, suggesting connection between conscious and unconscious. White lilies and roses grow by the poolside, both lunar flowers.

The Moon shines down upon the scene, revealing her three faces: new, full and old, which correspond to the three faces of woman: virgin, mother and hag. Mythically, each face can be compared to a goddess: for the new moon, Artemis the virgin moon goddess, or Persephone virgin goddess of the underworld; Demeter, the earth-mother goddess of the full moon; and Hecate, witch-enchantress goddess for the dark face of the moon. The three faces reveal the three aspects of femininity: the virgin who is full of potential waiting to be fulfilled; the mother whose potential is fulfilled; and the hag, whose potential has shrivelled up or been wasted.

The Moon is the mistress of the night, the womb to which men return each night to rest, sleep and dream. The Moon was once thought of as home of the dead, for it was believed that the souls of the dying would leave their bodies and be drawn up to the moon where they would be kept safe until the time was ripe for rebirth. The Moon was thus seen as both the womb that brings forth new life, and the tomb to which all life eventually returns. The Moon rules the waxing and waning rhythms of life, of tides and all natural cycles. The Moon also symbolizes feelings and emotions that are by nature volatile, nebulous and uncertain. She rules the realm of unconscious thought, dream and fantasy, and as the High Priestess signified the wisdom of the unconscious revealed in a controlled way, the Moon symbolizes the unconscious in its unpredictable and uncontrolled aspects. These aspects, when made conscious, can be transformed into wisdom. If the unconscious and conscious minds can function together harmoniously, the result is a well-integrated personality.

In a reading, The Moon usually points to a phase of fluctuation and change. It often indicates uncertainty and even illusion. It can also suggest that solutions to problems can be found through dreams and intuitions rather than logic and reason.

THE SUN

O nce again, after darkness there is light. The Sun is a cheerful and welcome image after the misty uncertainty of the Moon. A child wrapped in red banners is riding a powerful horse, the same horse that Death rode but this time it is white to symbolize life. A laurel hedge, representing success, forms a boundary to the fertile garden, which is rich with sunflowers, heliotrope and orange trees, all solar flowers and fruit. The Fool cannot help but respond with feelings of joy and optimism at the fresh-faced friendly child who greets him in the image of the Sun.

The fact that a child, rather than an adult figure, is depicted points to the chance that the Fool has to revert to a childlike state again so he can restart his inner or spiritual growth. White is the colour of life and purity of spirit, and red is the colour of desire and energy. The red cloak that the child is wrapped in may be symbolic of all the cloaks worn by the figures in the earlier Trumps, cast off and given to the child to wear in triumph; their lessons have been learned so they have no further need of them. The dazzling midday sun shines bright, with its rays both straight and wavy, indicating the dual nature of The Sun card, positive and negative. The dense laurel hedge represents the formation of the Fool's past life and his limitations. It stands for all he has learned and experienced so far; the pattern of experience, which has become a solid foundation from which he can now proceed.

The Sun has many mythical associations, the most obvious one being the sun god Helios, whose job it was to drive the chariot carrying the sun across the skies bringing light and heat to the earth. Another dimension of Helios is Apollo, born of Leto, goddess of the night. Apollo's shrine at Delphi was sacred to all goddesses of darkness. Apollo's twin sister was Artemis, the goddess of the Moon, and together they ruled day and night, twelve hours each. Apollo was also an archer, like his sister, and his fiery arrows could both heal sickness and cause sudden death to those who ran foul of him. He was often depicted with his famous lyre as the god of music, poetry and song. He was a god of form, shaping elusive aspects of the psyche into artistic expressions that are durable and permanent.

The Sun symbolizes the masculine capacity to impart form and structure. His influence gives form to the formless, shape to the shapeless. The Sun god presides over the arts as well as over the activity of the intellect, and man's rational capacity to impose order and coherence on the fluctuating moods of his experience. The Sun is a card of daylight, which, while it lasts, is a time for vigorous activity and clear perception. In this respect, the Sun complements the Moon, for if the Moon represents the unconscious in its murky darkness, the Sun is consciousness in all its bright lucidity. If the Moon signifies the feeling nature, the Sun stands for the capacity for thought. And as the Moon is formless, so the

Sun is form. The Sun, like the Moon, has its negative aspects. While form, structure, expression and articulation are things that can prove a great advantage, there are circumstances when they can be taken too far. It can be a mistake, for example, to attempt to structure and regulate feelings in accordance with logic. Air and fire, the masculine elements, can dry out water and earth. The sun can ripen fruit but it can also lay waste a desert. Water and earth, on the other hand, can drown or bury the volatile elements of air and fire. The elements must co-exist in nature and in the personality to achieve balance. If the Fool approaches the Sun with reverence and caution, he can richly benefit from this benevolent source of life and strength.

In a spread, this card represents energy and a source of strength.
The Sun stands for success, prosperity, happiness and true friends.
It seems to brighten all the cards surrounding it, adding a sense
of optimism and good cheer.

Judgement

Judgement is the penultimate stage of the Fool's journey. He has almost reached his goal with only this and the final card, The World, to encounter. The Judgement card depicts an angel appearing from the clouds, a halo of golden curls around his youthful face. He is blowing a mighty trumpet from which hangs a white banner emblazoned with a red cross. Three naked figures of a man, woman and child arise from their coffins, their arms outstretched. Their coffins float in a dark sea, which becomes increasingly lighter and calmer as it stretches out to the horizon. The image is one of joy and release. The points of the red cross on the white banner signify that the way to spiritual ascent is through the reconciliation of opposites, which then form a higher unity. The central crossing point of the two lines shows a joining together of all things that have been separate or separated. The naked figures illustrate more important symbolic detail. They are naked because they have thrown off their garments of worldliness in favour of spirituality. The figures appear to be rising from their graves: the coffins are open and they are free to climb out. The darkness of the sea and the tombs represents the dark underworld, life without initiation. The figures have undergone a spiritual rebirth; they died in order to find themselves and they are now ready to acquire the new life to which they are being summoned.

The angel blowing the trumpet could be St Michael, who functions as a guide of souls and whose trumpet is due to sound out on the Day of Judgement. Michael was one of the seven archangels who was said to guide the planets, his own special planet being Mercury. This takes us full circle and brings us back to Hermes, known to the Romans as Mercury, the guide of souls, whom the Fool first met at the beginning of his journey under the guise of the Magician. Indeed it was the Magician who started the Fool on his journey, led him unseen along the way, accompanied him on his descent into darkness and now leads him triumphantly towards the light, and his goal. Hermes is a god with many facets; he is the messenger of the gods, especially to Zeus, and arranges dealings between men and the gods. He is a guide to men on their journeys and in his role as trickster he could guide and mislead; help and hinder. However, in his role as psychopomp he acts as a powerful underworld god, guiding the souls of the dead to Hades but also summoning the dead back to life. According to myth, when the unpleasant King Tantalos decided to cook his own son and serve him to the gods at a feast as a joke, it was Hermes who reassembled the unfortunate young man and restored him to life. Hermes also freed a number of heroes, including Theseus and Heracles, who found themselves trapped in the underworld, and it was Hermes who guided Orpheus in and out of the underworld in search of his wife, Eurydice.

As its image suggests, Judgement is a card of summing-up, of balancing accounts and it is through this card that the Fool's progress is evaluated and assessed. Judgement may symbolize what, in Eastern thought, is called karma, the principle whereby man's actions produce their appropriate reward or punishment. In Western tradition, this is summed up by the phrase 'as you sow, so shall you reap'. Judgement reflects a process of self-appraisal, an honest and sincere attempt to come to terms with oneself and whatever resolutions one has found for inner conflict. It necessitates removing the veils through which man generally perceives himself and either over-estimates or under-estimates his efforts. After all, excessive modesty or self-recrimination is just as erroneous as excessive egotism or complacency. Judgement stresses the need to evaluate oneself and one's accomplishments at their true worth and though we condemn those who puff themselves up, we should also condemn those who, for whatever reason, sell themselves short. The card of Judgement marks the completion of the karmic cycle, in which reward or penalties are conferred in accordance with one's true worth.

In a reading, the Judgement card signifies the final settlement of a matter, a 'clean slate', paying off old debts and a preparedness for a new beginning. It indicates that things which have lain fallow will come to life, and reward for past effort will finally be forthcoming. It is a time for rejoicing and renewal.

THE WORLD

At last, the Fool arrives at The World, the final and most complex card in the Major Trumps. The enigmatic image portrays a dancing figure floating in a wreath of laurel tied with red ribbons, carrying a wand in each hand. The figure is draped in a purple sash and wears a gold crown. The four corners of the image reveal a bull, a lion, an eagle, and a man.

The World dancer's purple sash is the colour of wisdom and divinity and it is draped in such a way as to conceal sexual gender, for this figure represents a hermaphrodite, a symbol of unity between the sexes. The two wands indicate the duality the Fool has encountered so many times along his route, and now both are contained within the wreath. There has been a constant emphasis on two halves forming a whole, pairs and opposites combining to become one. The wreath of laurel is a symbol of victory, success and triumph, while the red ribbons stand for the joy of achievement. The crown denotes authority and power. The four creatures at each corner stand for the fixed signs of the zodiac and reflect the four seasons and elements: Bull, Taurus, Spring, Earth; Lion, Leo, Summer, Fire; Eagle, Scorpio, Autumn, Water; Man, Aquarius, Winter, Air. The World dancer represents the blending and unification of the opposites to create harmony and balance. The life work of the alchemists was to blend all four elements to create a perfect fifth, the quintessence. The oval shape of the wreath echoes both the figure zero, symbolizing all beginnings and endings, and the womb from which all life emerges.

Hermaphroditus, in Greek myth, was born to Hermes and Aphrodite, his name being composed from both of theirs. One version of the myth suggests he was born dual sexed, while in another version, Aphrodite gave him to the nymphs who lived in the forests of Mount Ida so they might raise him. When he reached the age of fifteen, he was noticed and desired by the nymph Salmacis who ruled the particular lake he decided to swim in. At first Hermaphroditus refused her advances being somewhat shy and modest, and only when he thought he was alone, did he dare plunge into the lake. However, Salmacis soon popped up beside him in the waters, kissing and embracing him. The more he struggled, the tighter she held on to him, and she cried out to the gods begging them never to allow him to be separated from her. The gods heard her prayer and merged their bodies together and from then on they were as one, neither man nor woman, and yet at the same time, both.

The World card symbolizes completion by showing oneness with self and nature. It represents an establishment of oneself in one's right place, in relation to the cosmos and as an expression of internal and external harmony. The individual is now at one with nature and the world; there is a sense of satisfaction and achievement at finding one's rightful place.

Realization of the World is the objective to which mystics have aspired from time immemorial. Jung calls it the Realization of the Archetype of the Self; Christianity calls it Beatitude; it is the supreme goal in Buddhist, Hindu and Taoist traditions as well as the goal to which the cabalists aspire. It involves the ultimate integration of self and the cosmos as well as unity, harmony and balance. Whether it is a viable expectation for the average individual is indeed questionable but, certainly, intimations of it can be offered and occasionally even achieved. The World card symbolizes a connection with the great mystic traditions that have constituted a common denominator between all the world's great religions and systems of philosophical thought from ancient times to the present day. At the moment of completion and perfection, all that remains is to start another whole journey. The oval wreath symbolizes the womb, and the central figure, the foetus, waiting to be born again as the Fool, so the procession of Trumps may begin again.

In readings, this card shows the completion of one phase or stage of life; it suggests success, harmony and triumphant achievement. It is the realization of a sought-after prize or goal, and implies the moment of satisfaction and joy that such a feat brings. For this moment, the World is at your feet.

⊷ The Court Cards ⊶

We now come to the final section of the Minor Arcana, namely the Court cards. The Court cards act as a link or bridge between the Major and Minor and are often considered to be quite complicated to interpret because they can symbolize a number of different things. For example, they could symbolize a particular type of person entering the seeker's life; they could represent an aspect of the seeker's own personality or they could indicate an actual event. This does obviously make it a bit difficult to decide how to read the Court cards, as there are no hard-and-fast rules. Practice and experience will certainly help a great deal, as well as looking at the overall layout of the cards and the seeker's question or situation. As always, the more personal the feelings and responses to each card are, the easier it will become to know how to interpret it in each particular case.

Some people find that linking the Court cards with astrological signs can give a deeper understanding of each figure's personality. My own personal astrological associations are that the Pages reflect the essence of the astrological elements themselves - Fire, Water, Air and Earth; the Knights reflect the mutable signs of the zodiac - Sagittarius, Pisces, Gemini and Virgo; the Queens reflect the fixed signs - Leo, Scorpio, Aquarius and Taurus; and the Kings reflect the cardinal signs - Aries, Cancer, Libra and Capricorn.

The Pages

Traditionally, the Pages are known as messengers, often represented as children, because they symbolize something embryonic or an aspect of the personality that is just beginning to develop. If they indicate an event, it is usually associated with the beginning of something new and undeveloped. As with the pip cards, the basic energy of the Page is reflected through the suit and the element of that suit.

Page of Wands

A number of symbols recur through the suit of Wands, one of which is the salamander, that fiery creature believed to live in the flames of fire. Others are the sunflower, a solar plant, the sun and little flames, which stand like buds on the stems of all the wands. The Page of Wands stands proudly holding his wand firmly in his right hand, the side of action. He looks out over the vast horizon and although he stands still, it is clear that action and movement will soon follow. Tiny

PAGE *of* WANDS

suns decorate his tunic and a salamander is engraved on his breastplate. If he represents a child or young person in a spread, it may be someone with a quick, intuitive, enthusiastic personality. A key point to remember about the Pages is their potential. A fiery Page represents the potential for creative possibilities, those small ideas that may grow into something substantial; after all, it only takes a spark to ignite a massive blaze. In a reading, if the seeker is trying to develop qualities of enthusiasm and optimism within him- or herself, this card can be a helpful one. In terms of representing an event, the Page may be a bearer of good news, glad tidings, a yearning for growth and a desire for knowledge, along with the opportunity to achieve this.

Page *of* Cups

PAGE *of* CUPS

The decorative imagery and themes that run through the suit of Cups are fish, mermaids and water. The fish is a symbol of creative imagination, and the element of water represents the feelings and the depth of the unconscious mind. The colours of the Page of Cups are soft pink and blue, reflecting the sweet and gentle characteristic of this card. The Page of Cups is a young man wearing a pink tunic embroidered with tiny blue fish. He is holding a golden cup with great care and tenderness, watching as a fish emerges from it cautiously, symbolizing the birth of creative imagination and new life. The landscape is green and fertile and the youth stands near a pool, indicating the element of water. If the Page in a spread is indicative of a young person, he stands for a sensitive, kind-natured type with strong artistic or even psychic talents. The Page of Cups may indicate these qualities, albeit in embryo, in the seeker. He may bring news of a birth, perhaps the birth of a child or of new feelings and attitudes. For example, if a seeker had been hurt and was afraid to trust emotionally, this card could indicate the fragile new beginnings in starting to trust again.

Page *of* Swords

Airy images dominate the suit of Swords: clouds, birds and butterflies. Blue, grey and purple are the colours that recur in this suit. The Page of Swords stands on guard, as if ready to defend himself against attack. He brandishes his sword high over his head; there are clouds in the sky, though not storm clouds, and birds fly high above them. He wears a blue tunic decorated with butterflies, and even the sleeves of his boots are appliquéd with

PAGE *of* SWORDS

tiny butterflies. It is clear that this card reflects the element of air. If the Page of Swords represents a young person, he could stand for a somewhat ruthless character, clever and intelligent but lacking in compassion for others. The Page of Swords isn't necessarily malicious but may evaluate things with logic rather than feeling. He may indicate one who has a strong will, yet who is cold and calculating. All the Pages can represent children, and in this card we may see how children use gossip and chatter as a means of communication and learning. In its best light the Page of Swords stands for the young mind stirring and expanding, and indicates a thirst for knowledge and mental stimulation. At worst, he stands for one who enjoys gossip or spreading rumours.

PAGE *of* PENTACLES

Indications of nature's bounty are the main themes that run through the earthy suit of Pentacles. In the Page these are shown by the new growth in the fields and the rabbit, symbol of fertility, bounding over the furrows. The greens and browns of the suit reflect the colours of nature; the overall impression of this image is one of calm patience. The Page of Pentacles stands still and straight, holding a pentacle firmly with both hands. The other Pages show a sense of movement; they look

PAGE *of* PENTACLES

ready to act, while this Page seems content to wait for the earth to produce fruit in its own time. This suit is associated primarily with earthly possessions or material goods, so this Page indicates a young person who respects such things, and takes good care of his worldly belongings and assets. He represents one who is prudent and cautious, hard-working and diligent, though perhaps rather solemn sometimes. If the seeker is trying to develop a sense of material value or worth, or perhaps wishes to start a business venture even on a small scale, this is a good card. As an event, the Page of Pentacles may signify an opportunity to make money, usually starting from the bottom but with plenty of promise for the future.

The Knights

We now come to the Knights, symbols of movement and action. The Knights stand for youth, although they are more advanced than the Pages. They are all seekers, searching through desert, ocean, sky or field to reach their chosen goal. Astrologically, the Knights represent the mutable signs.

Knight *of* Wands

A handsome knight on a fine steed gallops across desert-like terrain. He wears a cloak embroidered with suns, symbolizing the warmth of fire, and his horse's harness is trimmed with salamanders, denoting the fiery element. The single red feather stands for truth. The distant pyramids stand for knowledge and ancient wisdom. The Knight of Wands has an air of purpose and confidence about him, as he holds his Wand, symbol of creative energy, up high. He is connected with Sagittarius, the mutable fire sign. This young man has splendid ideas and a fine sense of adventure; he would make a generous and warm friend or lover, although he is inclined to be unpredictable and hasty in judgement. He has a good sense of fun. However, on a more serious note, he is a seeker of meaning and higher purpose, as in astrology Sagittarius stands for higher learning and interests of a philosophical or spiritual nature. If he stands for an event, it is usually a change of residence or a long journey, possibly even immigration. Sagittarius rules the ninth house of the zodiac, which is also connected with journeys.

Knight *of* Cups

The Knight of Cups, although as handsome as the Knight of Wands, proceeds in a much calmler fashion. His elegant white horse moves slowly and deliberately alongside a wide river, signifying the water element. His horse's harness is decorated with fish as is his tunic, denoting feelings, and his helmet is winged to represent his spiritual aspirations. He is connected with Pisces, the mutable water sign of the zodiac. If he stands for a person, it would be a refined, artistic, high-principled youth, quite possibly an idealist or someone seeking perfection. The Knight of Cups is traditionally known as the lover, or the one who offers, and he,

KNIGHT *of* CUPS

much like the Arthurian Knights of the Round Table, is on a quest for truth, beauty and love, and nothing will deter him from this search. He is 'in love with love' and his high principles encourage him to aim high in all respects, although he is often disappointed as a result. If he stands for an event, it may be a proposal of marriage, a proposition in the field of art, or even a rival in love.

KNIGHT *of* SWORDS

KNIGHT *of* SWORDS

The Knight of Swords dashes across the card, his horse's legs outstretched, its mane flying in the wind. The emphasis is on speed; the swift action of the wind is pictured often in the imagery of this suit. In the background, the trees are bent and the Knight leans back in his seat, his sword poised for battle. His horse's blanket is decorated with birds and the harness with butterflies as symbols of the air element. In astrological terms, the Knight of Swords can be connected with the mutable air

sign of Gemini. The Knight of Swords is a curious mixture, for he has an attractive, magnetic personality and easily draws attention and affection from others, although he often has less need of them than they have of him. Thus, there is a somewhat ruthless streak in him, although he is not intentionally cruel or malicious. He has a brilliant mind and good business judgement, and tends to get on well in his career. Gemini is the sign known for teaching, lecturing, communicating and education in general, as it is ruled by Mercury, the trickster. A person represented by this card would be someone who is full of intellectual flexibility and curiosity, is interested in everything, is volatile and changeable yet is also easily bored. As an event, the Knight of Swords may represent a situation that gets started swiftly amid great excitement but dies down almost as quickly, often leaving a certain amount of chaos in its wake. The Knight of Swords is known for stirring things up but disappearing before the difficulties can be pinned on him.

KNIGHT *of* PENTACLES

The Knight of Pentacles is noticeably different from the other three Knights in that his horse stands quite still. The Knight of Pentacles and his sturdy farm horse are depicted in a freshly ploughed field, quietly contemplating their surroundings. Oak leaves decorate his saddle blanket and harness, which connects the image with the earth element. This is a peaceful image and this Knight is a calm, gentle fellow with infinite patience and tolerance. He is reliable and trustworthy and will carry out a task to completion, no matter how long it may take. He always reaches his goal because he never gives up and always sets his sights on achievable rewards. The Knight of Pentacles plods on without frenzy or excitement, but his plodding wins him the reward. He is connected with the astrological sign of Virgo, and the mutable earth element. The Knight of Pentacles is kind to animals and children, and loves all things pertaining to nature. He indicates just such a person, unadventurous, but utterly reliable. Others often seek him out for his qualities of perseverance and capacity for honest hard work. As an event, he stands for the eventual positive outcome of a situation that has dragged on for a long while, or which has appeared fruitless.

THE QUEENS

In layouts, the Queens, like the other Court cards, can be taken for actual people or parts of the seeker's personality, but they tend not to indicate events in quite the same way as the Pages and Knights can sometimes do. The four Queens are connected with the four fixed signs of the zodiac.

QUEEN *of* WANDS

QUEEN *of* WANDS

A noble-looking woman, proud and tall, is seated upon a fine throne decorated with fiery salamanders and golden lions, symbol of Leo, the fixed fire sign. She holds the wand of power in her right hand, the side of action, and a sunflower in her left hand, the side of creativity. The wand is masculine and the sunflower is feminine; this figure displays the balance between the two. At her feet sits a cat, denoting her traditional role as queen of hearth and home. The Queen of Wands is full of the love of life; she can successfully run a home and family but still finds time and energy to vigorously pursue her own interests. She can have several projects in progress at one time yet never lets anything detract from the energy she puts into her home life. She is well liked and will always help her friends enthusiastically but, if crossed, she will fight as fiercely as any lioness. Her tireless versatility is a quality often sought after by others.

QUEEN *of* CUPS

The Queen of Cups is a very different queen indeed to the vibrant fiery Queen of Wands. The dreamy, fey Queen of Cups sits upon an elegant throne floating in the sea. The throne is made out of shells and decorated

with mermaids and dolphins. Her flowing silvery dress melts into the water. The ocean is a symbol of the depths of the feeling world over which she presides. She gazes into her golden cup as though in a trance. The Queen of Cups is connected with the fixed water sign Scorpio. She is queen of emotions and symbolizes a person who has reached a degree of understanding of her own emotional depth. She is comfortable in the realm of feelings, fantasy and imagination and is sensitive and creative. The Queen of Cups is often the object of love, attracting admiration for her qualities of gentleness and inner calm, yet she also has a certain air of containedness so common with fixed signs, which makes her quite fascinating. She is often highly artistic and creative, even mystical or prophetic. However, she is so deeply involved in her inner world that it makes relationships of an everyday or mundane nature strangely difficult for her. The Queen of Cups represents a sense of being in touch with her feeling world, so when this card appears in a reading it may mean that the seeker needs to pay attention to their inner world, too.

QUEEN *of* SWORDS

The Queen of Swords is a more austere figure, seated upright on a stone throne carved with an angel whose wings represent the spirit. Decorative butterflies also appear as symbols of the element air. Her cloak is made up of blue sky and clouds and she holds her sword upright as a symbol of justice and truth. A single bird flies high in a darkening sky, signifying the woman's ability to think clearly and take a higher view of things. In astrology, this Queen is connected with

Aquarius, the mutable air sign. Traditionally, the Queen of Swords represents a woman who has experienced sorrow, or who may be alone

through widowhood, divorce or separation. She may have loved and lost, but believes she will live to love again, and in the meantime bears her pain with courage and resignation. The Queen of Swords is a symbol of strong will and determination, a person who can bear whatever difficulties life may put in her way. Her dignity is admirable as is her ability to wait patiently for better times to come. Acquiring this Queen's qualities to bear suffering with strength can be supportive and helpful in times of loss and sorrow.

QUEEN *of* PENTACLES

The Queen of Pentacles sits contentedly and comfortably in a fertile garden, her throne decorated with bulls' heads, connecting this card with the fixed earth sign of Taurus. The garden is full of flowers, including roses, which are the sacred flower of Venus, goddess of beauty and the ruling planet of Taurus. The Queen's cloak is made of red roses, and a rabbit, symbol of fertility, sits by her feet. The Queen of Pentacles is practical and materialistic. She loves the good things in life and is prepared to work hard to get them, particularly those things that appeal to the five senses, such as good food, fine clothing, lovely fragrances, excellent music and beautiful surroundings. Having acquired these things, she is able to feel a sense of contentment and satisfaction. She accepts responsibility gladly and is fair and wise in business. This Queen may represent someone rich who accumulated wealth by working hard and tirelessly for material gain. She can indicate a helpful friend or employer, because she is generous with her good fortune and may signify help of a practical nature.

THE KINGS

The Kings, as partners to the Queens, stand for masculine energy, and authority within their own suits. They are dynamic and active and correspond to the cardinal signs in astrology.

KING *of* WANDS

KING *of* WANDS

The King of Wands leans forwards restlessly; he looks set for action. As a fiery king, his throne and robes are adorned with salamanders and lions, and the armrests are golden rams, symbol of Aries, the cardinal fire sign of the zodiac. The King of Wands is the master of wit and charm. He is warm and generous with a good sense of humour and a strong liking for fun. He can persuade anyone to do anything because he is so amusing and optimistic; he is the archetypal salesman who could sell the proverbial ice to the eskimos. The King of Wands is full of new ideas and has an abundance of vision and foresight. His hunches always seem to pay off and he will happily make instant decisions, even on major matters. However, he dislikes detail and gets easily irritated if his enthusiasm is challenged or curbed by the practicalities or realities of life. He has total trust in his world of ideas and intuition; he cheerfully rides on the crest of the waves of success and any failures are simply forgotten or dismissed as unimportant.

KING *of* CUPS

The King of Cups sits on a throne in slightly troubled seas. A fish, symbol of creative imagination, leaps joyfully out of the waves in the distance, but the golden fish around the King's neck seems an empty token compared to the lively fish of imagination prancing about play-

fully behind him. His robes do not touch the
water and he seems somewhat uncomfortable,
unlike the Queen, who merges into the waves
without effort. Astrologically, this card is connected with Cancer, the cardinal water sign. A
tiny crab, a symbol of Cancer, sits beside him. He
is the master of emotions and his mood can change
quickly, but there is something about the King of
Cups that suggests he is not fully connected with
his watery element. The masculine cardinal energy

of the King of Cups is conscious, active and intellectual and is therefore
not totally at ease in the realms of deep emotion. This King is often to be
found in the helping professions, traditionally in the church, law, medi-
cine or psychology, because of his desire to be united with his inner
feeling world even though it doesn't always come easily to him. He tends
to pay lip-service to feelings rather than fully experiencing them. If the
King of Cups appears in a spread, it may represent an aspect of the
seeker's personality, suggesting that it is time for him or her to get truly in
touch with his feelings.

King *of* Swords

The King of Swords stares straight ahead, his
sword tilted to the right, the side of action. His purple cloak is the colour of wisdom, and his throne
is carved with butterflies, the symbol of the element air. The King of Swords is connected with
the cardinal air sign of Libra, the sign of balance.
Like many Librans, the King of Swords loves
truth and justice, and deplores uncivilized and
barbaric behaviour. It is a card and sign that
enjoys and values harmony and beauty. The two
birds above him signify his duality of vision as he prizes fairness and
equality. The King of Swords is one who rules with justice, and has firm

moral convictions; he is deeply committed, both in friendship and in enmity. He is not easily swayed by pleas for mercy or compassion, unlike the King of Cups who is more likely to be soft hearted and sympathetic. The King of Swords judges harshly but with scrupulous fairness and from a logical standpoint. He is often found in positions of authority and is a much-respected and occasionally feared figure. He can be suspicious and over-cautious, the 'strong, silent type'. His qualities of strength of character, a sense of fairness and justice, are highly commendable as long as they can be tempered with compassion and empathy.

King *of* Pentacles

The King of Pentacles sits on a lavish throne wearing robes covered with bunches of grapes symbolizing the earth's sweetness and bounty. Vines covered in ripe fruit stand on either side of him, while a fine castle can be seen in the distance, symbolizing his earthly achievements and status. He holds an orb in one hand, a symbol of material attainment, and a pentacle in the other, denoting the earth's magic. He is connected with Capricorn, the cardinal earth sign, whose symbol is the mountain goat, the heads of which adorn the armrests on his throne. The King of Pentacles stands for someone who loves riches and is determined to amass as much wealth as possible. He is clever in business matters, a bit of a financial wizard, yet status and respect from the outside world is also very important to him. However, he is not corrupt in his love of riches and earns money through hard, patient effort, not unworthy or dishonest business dealings. This figure is pretty straightforward; he enjoys what he has, and is generous with it, gladly sharing the fruits of his labour with others. The quality of being content with what you have is actually quite rare, yet this simple lesson, so hard to learn, can be taught by the King of Pentacles.

Exercises for Part Three

⟶ The Major Arcana ⟵

Now that you have completed your detailed examination of the whole pack, finish off the guided fantasy exercises for the remaining Major Arcana cards using exactly the same procedure as you did in Parts One and Two. You will, therefore, be starting with Death and working through each card in turn: The Devil; The Tower; The Star; The Moon; The Sun; Judgement and The World. Take note of your feelings about each meeting with the image or figure on the card. Remember that the crucial part of this exercise is to allow yourself enough time to relax thoroughly and pay full attention to each character you meet. Lastly, think about yourself as the Fool, having finally completed your journey through the Major Arcana. When you come to The World card, compare your notes and feelings to the first exercise you did with the Fool, when you imagined yourself jumping off the precipice into the unknown. What have your learned? What difference has it made? Do you feel any different? If so, how? Let yourself answer these questions honestly and openly.

The next exercise is one to test your knowledge and progress in learning the meaning of the cards. Spread the whole pack out in front of you face down and pick a card at random. Turn it up and jot down all you can remember about the card without checking the book. Then compare your notes against what it says in the book. Do this for as many cards at a time as you can, eventually working your way through them all.

⟶ The Minor Arcana ⟵

Now turn to the Court cards and look at each one in turn. Try to imagine the personality of each character. Identify the figure that you feel is most like you, and the one who is least like you. Now try to match up the personality or character of each card with a family member or close friend.

Perhaps you find it useful to use the astrological associations, or try it the other way round – think of a friend or relative's zodiacal sign and then see how it matches up to the equivalent Court card figure. Try to connect each card with someone you know or an aspect of yourself. If you like, you can make up stories around the various suits or 'family' groups. Use your knowledge and understanding of the element to help you and compare the same figures from each suit; for instance, see how the energy of the Knights is revealed differently through the various elements. You will see how the mutability that is common to all four Knights feels different in each element. Now try this with the Queens and Kings and you will gradually start to distinguish between the different qualities of each rank and how they are expressed in each element. The effort you put into getting to know the cards intimately will be extremely useful as you progress.

Once you feel really comfortable with each of the images, their meanings and messages, you are ready for the fourth and final part of the study: mastering the art of interpretation.

PART FOUR

⇌ READINGS ⇌

Y ou are now ready to move on to the final section in which we will
examine some sample spreads. At this point, it may be useful to re-
emphasize your main objectives when reading the Tarot. As has already
been stated, many seekers will consult the Tarot when they are in a confused or unhappy state or when they are facing a difficult decision or
situation. They may come to you hoping for help and guidance but at the
same time think that they should reveal nothing to you as the reader, in
case it somehow influences the way you translate the sequence of cards.
This attitude can be rather counterproductive, for while the cards can
reflect something of the seeker's current situation, they cannot pinpoint
minute detail, so shared comment and dialogue can be very profitable.
The Tarot is not a fortune-telling computer; it is a method whereby the
reader can access unconscious knowledge, from which they might be
able to offer some guidance. Tarot reading is not to be confused with clair-
voyance. Some clairvoyants do use the Tarot, but they don't always read
the symbols accurately; they merely use them as a prop, in the same way
that the messages 'read' from a crystal ball, for instance, do not lie within
the ball but within the reader. The Tarot images are there to be inter-
preted, and of course some readers are better at interpretation than
others. It is a bit like playing the piano; although anyone can learn the
notes, some people are more musical and can interpret the music more
naturally and intuitively than others. However, by faithfully following
the exercises such as guided fantasy techniques, intuition can be developed and expanded.

How to Read the Cards

It is a good idea to experiment with different layouts until you find the format that suits you best. Please do not think that the spreads illustrated here are the only ones available. There are a great many to choose from; and, in addition, you could make up your own spreads. The term 'layout' refers to the various positions in which the cards are laid out, each relating to a specific area of life, such as relationships, work, finances. This gives a framework within which to work, and gives the readings a basic structure. The question of who shuffles the cards, the reader or seeker, is another of personal preference. Some readers hand the deck of cards to the seeker to shuffle and then deal the cards off the top of the pack. Others, myself included, prefer to do all the shuffling themselves and simply invite the seeker to select a certain number of cards from the pack, which I spread, face down, in front of them.

Again, as a personal preference, I use the Major and Minor Arcana separately for a couple of spreads and then mix them together for the final reading. I use the Minor Arcana only for the Celtic Cross reading (*see pages 149-52*) to gain a picture of the seeker's life in terms of career, relationships and so on. Then I use the Star spread (*see pages 153-5*), with the Major Arcana only, to go into greater depth and find a reflection of the seeker's inner life. If I still need more information, I then use either the Horseshoe spread (*see pages 146-8*) or the Tree of Life (*see pages 156-60*), using the Major and Minor Arcana mixed together. However, this is only my personal preference and I strongly encourage you to experiment until you find the way that you feel works best for you.

A useful question to put to your seeker is, 'What do you want to gain from this reading?', and to yourself, 'What seems to be the best course of action indicated by these cards for this person at this time?' It is worth remembering that seekers are often concerned that their reading may be 'bad' or they hope it will be 'good'. It is actually not possible to equate the Tarot with morally concrete statements like this; the Tarot cannot lay down such value judgements. What it can do is offer an overview of the situation the seeker is in and from there you must try to figure out the most constructive way to handle the energies, whether 'difficult' or 'easy'. Let's take an example. If Death comes up in a reading, a seeker who does not know much about Tarot may panic, assuming that it means they or someone dear to them is about to die. In this case, you could reassure them that this card does not indicate physical death, and encourage them to look at the aspect of themselves or their lives that has reached, or is about to reach, the end of its usefulness. Death brings an opportunity for new life, and this is to be welcomed, although it always requires a period of mourning; Death could appear before a marriage, signifying the end of single life, just as easily as it could before a divorce, which denotes the end of a marriage. If The Devil appears in a spread – another card that causes panic in uninitiated seekers – you could point out the positive opportunity that The Devil presents for bringing into consciousness those unconscious blocks or inhibitions that prevent growth.

As I stated at the start of this book, I don't read reversed cards but, as this is just my personal preference, I would encourage you to experiment with reversals. Try them out in your own spreads and see how you like working with them, always remembering that your intuition is invaluable and that there is no 'right' or 'wrong' way. This is why learning Tarot can be liberating for those who like to take risks and experiment, but frustrating for those who want to be given prescriptions and to be told exactly what to do.

Let us now look at some spreads using layouts for seekers who have kindly given me permission to use their readings and case histories.

The Five-card Horseshoe

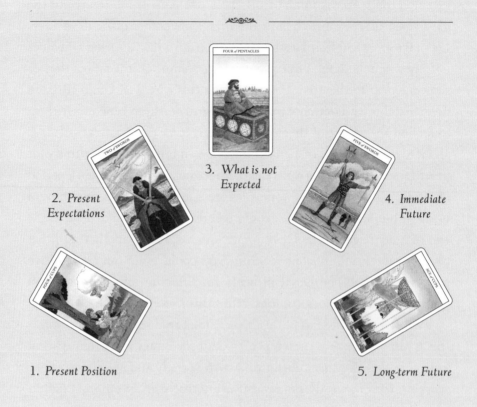

3. What is not
   Expected

2. Present
   Expectations

4. Immediate
   Future

1. Present Position

5. Long-term Future

Sally-Ann

*The first reading we are examining is for Sally-Ann, a twenty-seven-
year-old single woman living in a shared flat with another girl. She
came to see me for a reading because she faced a dilemma in her priorities.
Should she put her boyfriend or her career prospects first? For some time
she had been trying to get her own small business underway, rather
unsuccessfully, but had recently met a man with whom she was becoming
increasingly involved. She was unsure whether to put her work first, which
had been important for such a long time, or whether to abandon the
business project in favour of devoting more time and energy to
her new relationship.*

1. *Present Position* FOUR *of* CUPS

The Four of Cups represented Sally-Ann's current feelings and the situation surrounding her. The card shows a young man staring at three full cups before him. A fourth cup is being presented to him, but he doesn't seem happy with any of them. Sally-Ann seemed to be in a similar state of depression and confusion despite the fact that her situation was actually offering her a great deal. The Four of Cups indicated the lack of ability to choose, and although she had a lot of energy in potential, her state of mind ensured that none of it was channelled in a positive direction.

2. *Present Expectations* Two *of* SWORDS

The image on the Two of Swords shows a blindfolded woman carefully balancing two heavy swords. This reflected Sally-Ann's unwillingness to face up to her true desires. The figure has her hands crossed over her heart, as if Sally-Ann is afraid to accept her feelings for fear of being hurt. She was afraid to look at what she really wanted or felt (the water behind being her emotions) for she knew that it would entail making a decision (the rocks jutting above the water represent hard facts), which she felt too uncertain to face. This card aptly captured Sally-Ann's feeling of paralysis.

3. *What is not Expected* FOUR *of* PENTACLES

The Four of Pentacles symbolizes a fear of letting go of something that has been carefully acquired. It seemed that Sally-Ann didn't expect her inner feelings to be so fearful when considering both commitment to her boyfriend (she didn't realize how scared she was of losing her liberty) and the possibility of letting go of her business (even though it was rather shaky). She was unconscious of this aspect of the situation, and the position of the card gave her food for thought. She hadn't realized how much she wanted to keep everything just as it was, even though it was preventing growth and development on both fronts. And, indeed, because she felt so reluctant to change anything, it also made it impossible for her to gain or lose anything; the closed atmosphere of this card linked up with the message of the previous two cards: nothing ventured, nothing gained. In trying to keep everything as it was, she was actually preventing movement, which was why she felt so depressed and stuck.

4. *Immediate Future* FIVE *of* SWORDS

The Five of Swords, in the position of short-term future influences, seemed to suggest that it would be sensible for Sally-Ann to give up the present struggle, which was getting her nowhere, and to realize that she was tackling something that was too big for her. The more we talked, the clearer it became that her business, although dear to her heart, wasn't really financially viable. It had proved an expensive disappointment so far, and there was nothing to suggest things would improve in the near future without a massive injection of time and money, neither of which Sally-Ann felt she could afford. She felt that the message of this card was for her to stop fighting in vain and to try another route. This card counsels accepting limitations and acknowledging defeat, which must be done before moving on to something more profitable and feasible.

5. *Long-term Future* ACE *of* CUPS

The last card to be drawn in this spread was the Ace of Cups, overflowing with feelings, so future prospects for romance looked very good. It certainly seemed to imply light at the end of the tunnel for Sally-Ann, and showed that a strong loving union could provide strength and direction. The Ace of Cups indicates deep, positive emotions and the beginning of something promising that has the potential for joy and contentment.

I heard from Sally-Ann ten months later and she told me that she had given up her business, bought a flat with her boyfriend and had started a new job that she found interesting and stimulating. The relationship was working well and they were talking about the prospect of starting a family. She said that by giving up one thing she had gained a great deal.

The Celtic Cross

10. *The Outcome*

3. *What is Above You*

9. *Your Hopes and Fears*

6. *What is Before You*

1. *Present Position*

5. *What is Behind You*

8. *How Others See You*

4. *What is Beneath You*

7. *Where You Will Find Yourself*

Christopher

Christopher was a man of thirty-five, married with two boys, who came for a reading regarding his unhappy marriage and unsatisfactory working life. He was working as a solicitor in his uncle's firm, where he had been since graduation. He felt trapped there but also guilty about wanting to leave the family business. He had got married very young, to the daughter of a family friend, but it had become clear early on that the marriage was not one made in heaven. Christopher really wanted to change direction in life, both personally and professionally, but felt torn and guilty about the effect it would have on his whole family. I did a Celtic Cross spread using the Minor Arcana.

1. *Present Position* KINGS *of* SWORDS

The King of Swords in Christopher's present showed a strong figure of authority who is morally right and just, but may have little compassion for other people's feelings and problems. Christopher felt this described his uncle perfectly. His uncle was a powerful influence in Christopher's life; he was both respected and feared in the family and in the business world. Christopher was afraid that his uncle would not take kindly to his wish to leave both job and marriage, yet he longed to be free from the family obligations both at home and at work.

2. *What Crosses You* EIGHT *of* PENTACLES

Crossing Christopher's present position was the Eight of Pentacles, the card of the apprentice, which indicated the need to start again from the bottom, using skills and talents that might develop into a career. Christopher's hobby and passion was cooking, and he really wanted to run a small hotel or restaurant. He was considering taking a course in cooking and hotel management, with a view to starting a small business, possibly abroad. The card suggested that this was certainly possible, but because it 'crossed', it would be difficult or would take a long time.

3. *What is Above You* THREE *of* CUPS

This card signifies celebration and rejoicing. It suggests that some solution or resolution is to be found and therefore a sense of relief and happiness may be experienced. However, as the Threes all indicate an initial completion, I warned Christopher that much work would follow once the first stage was reached.

4. *What is Beneath You* EIGHT *of* WANDS

The Eight of Wands is a card denoting action and new direction, a time to be up and doing something, the end of delay and procrastination. Christopher told me he was feeling this kind of restlessness keenly at this time, and as this placement indicates what is already present at the base of his life, it seemed an appropriate card to spur him into action.

5. *What is Behind You* KNIGHT *of* PENTACLES

This card in the past position seemed, in Christopher's case, to represent his past action of plodding slowly but surely to a conclusion. He had been thinking of making a move for a very long time but could not quite find the courage to make a break, either careerwise or in his personal life. However, the Knight of Pentacles in his past seemed to suggest that the process had finally reached a conclusion. Christopher felt ready to take the plunge.

6. *What is Before You* SEVEN *of* WANDS

The Seven of Wands indicates stiff competition, but it also seemed to suggest that if Christopher were able to draw on his strength and determination to succeed, a change of profession or career would follow. He found it encouraging that this card seemed to be saying that he did not mind struggles or competition, as long as it was in a field of his own choosing.

7. *Where You Will Find Yourself* FOUR *of* WANDS

This card referred to how Christopher would find himself in the future and how he would feel about himself and his situation, so the card of 'harvest home' showed the possibility of Christopher reaping the benefit of what he has worked hard to achieve. As the Wands represent creative ventures, it could be that a new career would prove successful.

8. *How Others See You* TWO *of* SWORDS

The Two of Swords, the card of indecision and stalemate, represented Christopher's future environment, and how others would see him. It seemed to suggest that while one part of his dilemma would be solved, as indicated by the Four of Wands, another part would still lie in the balance. The Two of Swords suggests an inability to face facts because of the difficulties and changes that doing so would unleash.

9. *Your Hopes and Fears* TWO *of* CUPS

The Two of Cups denotes a comfortable balance, unlike the Two of Swords, which suggests tension. It is a card of reconciliation or new beginnings in relationships. Christopher said that, more than anything, he wanted to be able to stay on good terms with his wife and children but was very uncertain about the continuation of the marriage.

10. *The Outcome* EIGHT *of* CUPS

This card shows a man turning his back on eight carefully stacked cups, heading towards barren mountains in the distance. It could suggest that Christopher would leave behind all that he had worked so hard to achieve, disillusioned maybe, but possibly also able to face the reality of his situation.

To gain further clarification, I then did a spread for Christopher using just the Major Arcana and he chose the following cards:

The Star Spread

7. *The Top of the Matter*

6. *Conscious Influences and Desires*

5. *Unconscious Influence*

4. *The Heart of the Matter*

3. *Intellect and Career*

2. *Emotions and Relationships*

1. *The Root of the Matter*

1. *The Root of the Matter* DEATH

The Death card, in Christopher's present position, indicated a time for change, transformation, endings and new beginnings. Both internally and externally, it seemed necessary for him to let go of the old ways and values, which were stifling and unproductive, and allow new things to be born. Death in the reading indicated that the time was ripe to set this process in motion, and although it would be painful, it would nevertheless provide a clear way for Christopher to build a new life of his own.

2. *Emotions and Relationships* THE WORLD

The World is a very encouraging card to appear in the sphere of emotions, for it indicates a goal is reached and a sense of wholeness achieved. Combined with card 5, The Hanged Man, it seems to suggest that a sacrifice has to be made to allow a happy and beneficial outcome emotionally.

3. *Intellect and Career* THE EMPEROR

Opposite the card for the feelings, which often describes relationships, the card for the intellect usually corresponds with working life. The Emperor shows a solid, stable influence, which could mean that Christopher will find the strength of character to build a career for himself rather than relying on his family. The Emperor, after all, teaches the Fool to be a man in his own right, and this may mean he will do the same for Christopher.

4. *The Heart of the Matter* THE HERMIT

The centre of the spread is an important position, for the whole reading seems to revolve around it. The Hermit shows a need for inner contemplation and patient self-examination. It is a time for withdrawal and for carefully thinking things through. I suggested that some counselling or psychotherapy might help Christopher to understand the complexities of his current situation, rather than rushing into changing things.

5. *Unconscious Influence* THE HANGED MAN

In the position signifying that which lies beneath the surface and is about to emerge, is The Hanged Man. He indicates that a sacrifice must be made in order to gain something of greater value. Christopher felt he understood this card well, as he knew a conscious decision would have to be made by him alone. The essence of The Hanged Man is that the sacrifice is voluntary and made without outside pressure. Christopher had, to date, lived his life according to social and family dictates and now knew he must start making his own decisions if he was to gain self-respect.

6. *Conscious Influences and Desires* JUDGEMENT

What is 'wanted consciously' is renewal, rebirth and rejuvenation. At last, it seems, Christopher's potential will have an opportunity to come to light and be developed. The image of the dead rising and coffins opening to reveal talents hitherto unexplored is exciting. After Death comes resurrection, and Judgement triumphantly indicates the new life and opportunities. The Judgement is 'karmic', suggesting that past efforts will be rewarded.

7. *The Top of the Matter* THE LOVERS

The appearance of The Lovers card reinforced the idea that Christopher would have to make an important choice for himself. The Lovers often refers to relationships, so it seemed that he would have to make a careful assessment of his marriage and decide what to do about it. As there was no third party involved he would have to make the decision alone. The Lovers could indicate a new relationship or choices made regarding his marriage.

Following this reading, Christopher left his job, sold everything and moved to France with his wife and family to manage a small hotel. He made one change in his life but decided to give his marriage another chance. He felt liberated by his change of career and so felt more able and willing to work on his marriage, which had somehow been associated with his unhappiness at work.

The Tree of Life

1. *Spirituality*

3. *Difficulty*

2. *Responsibility*

5. *Opposing Matters*

6. *Achievement*

4. *Helpful Matters*

8. *Communication and Career*

9. *Unconscious Foundation*

7. *Emotional Relationships*

10. *Home and Family*

Diana

Diana, a young woman in her early thirties, came for a reading when she was in the midst of changing her job and about to get married and move house. She was understandably finding life pressured and felt anxious to learn how these major decisions would turn out. The reading unfolded as follows.

1. *Spirituality* ACE *of* PENTACLES

The first card Diana drew was the Ace of Pentacles, in the position for spiritual matters. This card suggested that a new beginning with firm foundations was the framework for her spiritual life to grow in. It seemed she felt comfortable with her inner beliefs and philosophies, and, because this card is usually connected with material wealth, yet turned up in the position for spiritual matters it seemed to indicate that she was 'wealthy' in her spiritual life. Diana confirmed that firm spiritual beliefs lay at the base of her life and offered her a good deal of comfort.

2. *Responsibility* Two *of* WANDS

The second card in the reading was the Two of Wands, in the position of responsibility. This card hints at movement and change. It shows a merchant standing on the ramparts of his castle, looking longingly out to sea. It suggests a desire to grow and expand and a wish to be getting on with life. A change or move is indicated. Diana told me how much she wanted to get everything sorted out: the purchase of the new home finalized, her promotion at work settled and the wedding smoothly organized. She was anxious to move on from her present position into her new life, and claimed she was more than willing to undertake the extra responsibility.

3. *Difficulty* TEN *of* CUPS

The Ten of Cups illustrates the ultimate of happiness in family life. The image is of a happy couple watching their children playing, and shows a life of promise and joy. However, it is placed in the position of difficulty, so although these good things were available to Diana because the card appeared in the reading, it also indicated that getting them may prove more difficult and challenging then she currently anticipated. Her marriage will prove fruitful, but she will have to work hard at it. Diana admitted that she was so absorbed in the details of the house purchase and wedding plans that she had not been paying much attention to the relationship itself.

4. Helpful Matters JUSTICE

The calming, balancing influence of Justice in the position of 'Helpful Matters' seemed extremely supportive in the midst of all the changing and rearranging that Diana's life was going through. Justice is the card of logical clear thinking, and an impartial perspective could help Diana work through her tasks steadily. Justice's clarity of vision could help prevent things from getting out of proportion.

5. Opposing Matters JUDGEMENT

Judgement, the card of new life and rebirth, falling in the position of 'Opposing Matters', shows that what is desired and appropriate can also be problematic. Judgement shows the opening up of skills and talents, which may have applied to Diana's promotion at work, and although she was pleased about it, it nevertheless added pressure to her already full schedule. The new challenges offered by Judgement showed that Diana's life was progressing positively, but she needed to remember that any change would inevitably involve a certain amount of stress, which she would have to accept.

6. Achievement FIVE of PENTACLES

The Five of Pentacles is a card meaning difficulties in financial matters. In the position of 'Achievement', as Diana prepared to buy a house and change jobs, this card warned that she might be at risk of spreading herself too thinly. In the card, two beggars stand in the snow, seemingly oblivious of the light flowing from the window above them. They are unaware that help is at hand, and Diana took this image as a warning that she was in danger of overstretching herself and becoming emotionally and possibly even financially impoverished. She was the major breadwinner of the couple and paying the mortgage depended largely on her salary, so she did feel under pressure. She took the church window to represent the need to draw on her spiritual resources for strength and support.

7. *Emotional Relationships* KNIGHT *of* SWORDS

As the reading unfolded, alongside the encouraging aspects that the earlier cards indicated, more factors began to emerge about Diana's inner fears and concerns. Firstly, there was the worry of the financial state of affairs represented by the Five of Pentacles, and then the Knight of Swords appeared in the sphere of relationships. I asked whether the Knight bore any similarity to her fiancé, but Diana said no. As we tried to place the significance of the Knight of Swords in this position, Diana told me about her former boss with whom she had had a complicated relationship and who reminded her of the characteristics of the Knight of Swords. Although Diana had not seen him for a while, he had phoned her unexpectedly a couple of days before the reading and he had not been pleased to hear the news of her forthcoming wedding. Diana felt uneasy at his response and was secretly afraid that he might try to make trouble for her. She had been heavily influenced by him in the past and did not want him to alter her decisions or feelings by his disapproval.

8. *Communication and Career* TEN *of* WANDS

The warning trend set in motion by the previous few cards seemed to continue in the next card, which referred to Diana's working life. The image shows a figure burdened by wands, carrying them awkwardly and with great difficulty. It seemed an appropriate message for Diana not to take on too much workwise, and to try to spread out her jobs in the easiest way possible. She told me that she knew she ought to delegate more at work, but found it difficult as she hated not doing everything herself, so was constantly getting caught out by having more to do than she could reasonably cope with. The image of the card helped her to clarify what she was doing to herself however, and she resolved to try to change that pattern.

9. *Unconscious Foundation* EIGHT *of* CUPS

On an unconscious level, it seemed that Diana wasn't fully aware of how much was actually changing, and while on the face of it the changes were positive and desired, they also brought with them a certain amount of stress and anxiety. The Eight of Cups illustrated the fact that Diana was leaving behind both her single life and a familiar, stable job and travelling towards the unknown mountain of marriage and the job that awaited her in the future. She felt it a relief to find words to articulate the concerns, as she had previously felt that to admit any fear would mean she was doing the wrong thing. It helped her to allow herself to acknowledge that she was happy and excited as well as nervous and fearful.

10. *Home and Family* ACE *of* CUPS

The final card in Diana's reading was the Ace of Cups. The reading seems to have come full circle from one Ace to another. The card shows a home life that is happy and loving and suggests that, through all the difficulties Diana had to encounter, she would be able to experience major life moves and come to grips with them, resulting in an emotionally satisfying relationship. The cards seemed to map out the pitfalls to be avoided, the difficulties to be made conscious and finally seemed to suggest the potential for love and emotional fulfilment.

The Celtic Cross

10. *The Outcome*

3. *What is Above You*

9. *Your Hopes
and Fears*

6. *What is
Before You*

1. *Present Position*

2. *What
Crosses You*

5. *What is
Behind You*

8. *How Others
See You*

4. *What is Beneath You*

7. *Where You
Will Find Yourself*

Emma

I did this Celtic Cross reading for Emma, aged thirty six, who came to see me for advice about her career. She was working in an investment bank, and although she was competent, made good money and had good prospects, she wasn't enjoying the work. She found the 'cut and thrust' unappealing and wanted to find something that involved working closely with people and their personal, rather than financial, needs. She was considering retraining, perhaps as a teacher, social worker or counsellor, but was unsure about the wisdom of such a move. Emotionally, she felt quite low as an important relationship had recently ended, so she was also interested in future prospects for her personal life.

1. *Present Position* PAGE *of* WANDS

The card signifying Emma's present position showed the beginnings of new creative or imaginative ideas, with the possibility of opportunities arising. The Page of Wands often indicates new interests and pursuits and, in Emma's case, it seemed to suggest that she was ready to follow leads on a new career path.

2. *What Crosses You* TEN *of* SWORDS

The Ten of Swords crossing Emma showed that something had ended, but, as the position was 'crossing', it was still concerning her. Emma felt that it was both the relationship ending and her waning interest in her work that was causing her to seek a change of direction. The graphic depiction of the man lying on the ground with swords in his back signifies the end of something; however, the sun rising in the distance gives the message of new life. The card means that something is seen for what it is truly worth, and this could be Emma's job. She had thought that her choice of career would result in a long-term commitment but had become increasingly disillusioned as, although it was materially beneficial, it gave her little personal satisfaction.

3. *What is Above You* Seven *of* Pentacles

The Seven of Pentacles suggested that Emma needed to decide whether to continue with her established and successful work or turn to something new and untried. There were obvious pros and cons to both, and it seemed that she should take her time to decide which was right for her.

4. *What is Beneath You* Two *of* Cups

The card of harmony and balance in relationships was in the base of the reading, revealing that some sort of reconciliation could be reached in Emma's relationship. Even if the romance may not be rekindled, which Emma hoped it could be, the Two of Cups suggested that, at least, a good friendship could emerge.

5. *What is Behind You* Three *of* Wands

This card seemed to symbolize Emma's past efforts in working steadily towards a certain level in her career, thinking that when she had reached it she would be satisfied. However, Three is the number of initial, rather than final, completion, so Emma reached that level only to discover that her horizons had changed and expanded, and that there were now other things that interested her which she had not previously considered.

6. *What is Before You* Page *of* Swords

The card describing the immediate future is the airy Page of Swords. Pages describe new beginnings and the Swords is the suit of the intellect, so it seemed that Emma's thinking was changing and she needed to allow herself the time and space to develop new ideas. Anything new is vulnerable and new ideas are often in danger of being crushed or ridiculed, so Emma needed to be careful about who she chose to discuss her innermost thoughts with. It also acted as a warning against gossip or rumours, which could brew up at work if she wasn't careful.

7. *Where You Will Find Yourself* QUEEN *of* WANDS

The card signifying Emma's future position is the Queen of Wands, who is sometimes called 'queen of hearth and home'. She is an active figure with enough energy to give to both home and career. She is dynamic and creative in business but also warm hearted and generous personally. Emma indicated that it would be her ideal to have both a family and a satisfying career.

8. *How Others See You* PAGE *of* CUPS

The third Page card in the spread showed that many new possibilities were ready to open up. The Page of Cups suggested that new feelings would emerge and her heart would slowly heal so that she could love and trust again. This card brings the potential for birth, be it a child, a relationship or a new way of feeling. The appearance of so many Pages seemed significant, particularly in view of the way Emma was feeling at the time of the reading.

9. *Your Hopes and Fears* Two *of* SWORDS

The Two of Swords in this position suggested that Emma was fearful of remaining stuck and indecisive. This card is one of stalemate and deliberate blindness to current circumstances. She hoped that she would find the courage to change, but was afraid that her timid side might let her down.

10. *The Outcome* EIGHT *of* CUPS

The fears surrounding the Two of Swords seemed unfounded, as the final card, the Eight of Cups, shows a figure walking away from a carefully constructed situation in search of something new. It seemed that Emma would indeed find the strength to change her direction but, with the numerous Pages in the reading, it would take time for things to unfold. It was clearly important to take the time as once the decision was made it would be final.

I then did a Major Arcana reading for Emma, as follows:

The Star Spread

7. *The Top of the Matter*

6. *Conscious Influences and Desires*

5. *Unconscious Influence*

4. *The Heart of the Matter*

3. *Intellect and Career*

2. *Emotions and Relationships*

1. *The Root of the Matter*

---

1. *The Root of the Matter* THE HIGH PRIESTESS

As the Root of the Matter, the High Priestess reveals potential that is unfulfilled and uncharted terrain waiting to be discovered. This card suggests a need to allow the potential to slowly emerge. Emma needed to be able to trust the intuitive process that was already at work; the High Priestess symbolizes secret wishes and dreams being revealed so this seemed an appropriate card to start off the spread. The High Priestess suggests an interest in, and a search for, knowledge of a complex and powerful nature, especially where related to the unconscious mind. It seemed that the high-powered masculine world of banking and finance would not sit comfortably with Emma's current inner growth process.

2. *Emotions and Relationships* THE FOOL

The Fool, appearing in the position for emotions and relationship issues, indicated the need to take risks. It seemed the time was coming for Emma to consider jumping off the edge of an emotional precipice. In Emma's case I felt it heralded a new relationship arriving on the scene. She would have to let go of her fears and self-protective instincts and take the plunge. Having been quite badly betrayed in her previous relationship, it was clearly not going to be easy for her to trust again, but The Fool's presence gave her some enthusiasm and she was determined to try to overcome her fears.

3. *Intellect and Career* TEMPERANCE

The position for work life was dominated by Temperance, a gentle card suggesting a time for compassion and cooperation. It seemed that Emma's current interest and inclination was towards helping people in emotional ways rather than financial ones, and that the presence of Temperance in this position echoed this shift. Temperance certainly indicated a feeling of harmony in her working life.

---

4. *The Heart of the Matter* THE LOVERS

The Heart of the Matter position is important in that it indicates what is most crucial in the spread. It seems that an important decision is looming and it must be carefully considered. The Lovers indicate a choice, sometimes about relationships but not exclusively. It may have transpired that a new relationship would come into play, but it may also have referred to Emma's career dilemma. Choices are a difficult part of life and always involve giving something up; however, they also involve gaining something. Those were the issues that Emma had to struggle with at the time of the reading.

5. *Unconscious Influence* THE WHEEL OF FORTUNE

The Wheel of Fortune in the position of Unconscious Influence shows that a new chapter is about to start in Emma's life. As the Wheel turns, she will have a new opportunity to take more responsibility for her life and to make positive future plans. The Wheel of Fortune brings change and marks the commencement of a new cycle. A good motto for this card is 'The old order changeth.'

6. *Conscious Influences and Desires* THE MOON

The shifting, moving influence of The Moon shows the uncertainty and mood swings connected with Emma's conscious desires. I suggested that the more she became aware of what was beneath the surface, as symbolized by the crab crawling out of the pool, the easier it would be for her to make up her mind on a course of action. The Moon signifies a time when dreams and intuitions should be taken seriously and focused on. Emma didn't want to change her life abruptly on a whim, yet nor did she feel inclined to wait in the dark. Both The High Priestess at the base of the reading and The Moon gave a similar message: something was gestating in the womb of the unconscious mind and it would take time and trust for it to come to fruition. Although the lack of clarity was frustrating, it was a process that Emma would have to endure in order not to rush into the wrong thing simply to avoid the uncomfortable wait for the solution to emerge.

7. *The Top of the Matter* JUDGEMENT

The message of rebirth and renewal as a concluding card shows that a cycle would be completed and rewards would be reaped from the seeds of past effort. At the appropriate time, Emma's unrevealed and unfulfilled potential would come to consciousness and be brought to fruition, as portrayed by the dead rising up from their graves. Emma needed to give herself the right time and space to allow the energies of the cards to unfold gradually and, if she did, she would be sure of which direction to take and she would be able to see her new life follow that lead.

Final Exercises

N ow that you have worked your way through the cards and exercises and have looked at the sample spreads, it is time to put what you have learned so far into practice. Experiment on yourself and your friends as you begin to develop your own style and method of reading. You can continue with the guided-fantasy exercises, which will yield interesting results indefinitely. In fact it can be fascinating to compare and contrast the result of your first exercise with the same exercise performed a year later. There is no limit to the number of times you do the same exercise and you can be sure that each time will be different. You may find it useful to record your readings so that you can refer back to them: a few templates for this purpose are offered overleaf.

When you begin reading the cards, don't be afraid to make mistakes. Try to put the book aside and work directly with the card imagery. Study the pictures and let them talk to you; only refer to the book if you get seriously stuck. In the first instance try to find the interpretations for yourself. If you have followed the exercises faithfully, this will not be hard.

And, when doing readings, don't be afraid to involve your seeker; they will have input into the reading and can help you to make sense of it. You are not expected to be clairvoyant so it doesn't matter if you ask your seeker questions or for clarification.

So having come full circle, from the Fool to the World, it is time for you to continue on your own, starting, as always, as the Fool, about to commence the journey all over again.

We shall not cease from exploration
And the end of all our exploring
Will be to arrive where we started
And know the place for the first time.

T. S. ELLIOTT, Four Quartets

Notes on Your Own Readings

DATE .... READING FOR..

SITUATION ....

....

SPREAD USED ....

CARD POSITIONS

....

....

....

....

....

....

OVERALL ANALYSIS

....

....

....

....

....

....

....

....

....

DATE .... READING FOR...

SITUATION ....

....

SPREAD USED ....

CARD POSITIONS

....

....

....

....

....

....

OVERALL ANALYSIS

....

....

....

....

....

....

....

....

....

DATE .... READING FOR ....

SITUATION ....

....

SPREAD USED ....

CARD POSITIONS

....

....

....

....

....

....

OVERALL ANALYSIS

....

....

....

....

....

....

....

....

....

DATE .... READING FOR..

SITUATION ....

....

SPREAD USED ....

CARD POSITIONS

....

....

....

....

....

....

OVERALL ANALYSIS

....

....

....

....

....

....

....

....

....

DATE .... READING FOR ....

SITUATION ....

....

SPREAD USED ....

CARD POSITIONS

....

....

....

....

....

....

OVERALL ANALYSIS

....

....

....

....

....

....

....

....

....

Bibliography

Banzhaf, Hajo. *Tarot Handbook*, US Games Systems Inc., 1994

Banzhaf, Hajo. *Tarot and the Journey of the Hero*, Red Wheel/Weiser, 2000

Cavendish, Richard. *The Tarot*, Michael Joseph, 1975

Court de Gebelin, Antoine. *Le Monde Primitif Analysé et Comparé avec le Monde Moderne*, Paris, 1781

Decker, R., and Dummett, M. A. *History of the Occult Tarot 1870-1970*, Gerald Duckworth & Co. Ltd, 2002

Douglas, Alfred. *The Tarot*, Penguin Books, 1973

Encausse, Gérard, 'Papus'. *Le Tarot des Bohémiens*, Paris, 1889

Gray, Eden. *The Tarot Revealed*, Inspiration House, 1958

Huson, Paul. *The Devil's Picturebook*, Abacus, 1971

Huson, Paul. *Mystical Origins of the Tarot*, Destiny Books, 2004

Kaplan, Stuart R. *The Encyclopedia of Tarot: Vol. 1*, US Games Systems Inc., 1978

O'Neill, Robert V. *Tarot Symbolism*, Fairway Press, 1986

Pollack, Rachel. *Seventy-Eight Degrees of Wisdom*, The Aquarian Press, 1983

Tilley, Roger. *Playing Cards*, Octopus Books, 1973

Waite, A. E. *The Pictorial Key to the Tarot*, Rider, 1971

Weston, Jessie. *From Ritual to Romance*, Anchor Books, 1957

Yates, Frances, A. *The Art of Memory*, Routledge & Kegan Paul, 1966

About the Author

꧁☙꧂

Juliet Sharman-Burke is a practising analytic psychotherapist. She has been using the Tarot and astrology for over twenty years, and has taught both subjects since 1983. She has written several books on the Tarot, including *The Beginner's Guide to Tarot*, *The Mythic Tarot Workbook*, *Understanding the Tarot*, and *Mastering the Tarot*. She is also co-author with Liz Greene of the bestselling classic deck *The Mythic Tarot* and *The Mythic Journey*.

Acknowledgements

꧁☙꧂

Thanks to Rich Leigh for his invaluable encouragement with this book and over the years; to Deb Buxton for her help in compiling and typing the correspondence course out of which this book grew; to my father Gerald Burke for his help in editing and to Sandra Wastiage whose practical support was so much appreciated and who, sadly, did not live to see publication.

And many thanks to Ian Jackson, Nick Eddison, Katie Golsby and Barbara Levy for their ongoing help and encouragement.

EDDISON · SADD EDITIONS
Editorial Director   Ian Jackson
Editor   Katie Golsby
Proofreader   Peter Kirkham
Art Director   Elaine Partington
Mac Designer   Brazzle Atkins
Production   Sarah Rooney